17.95

(239)

D1357191

# The Sacrifice We Offer

# The Sacrifice We Offer

## The Tridentine Dogma and its Reinterpretation

DAVID N. POWER, O.M.I.

T. & T. CLARK LIMITED
59 GEORGE STREET
EDINBURGH

Copyright © David N. Power, O.M.I., 1987

Typeset by C. R. Barber & Partners, Fort William,
printed and bound by Billing & Son, Worcester,

for

T. & T. CLARK LTD, EDINBURGH.

First printed 1987.

British Library Cataloguing in Publication Data

Power, David N.
The sacrifice we offer: the Tridentine
dogma and its reinterpretation.
1. Lord's Supper—Catholic Church—
History
I. Title
234'.163'09031      BV823

ISBN 0-567-09445-6

# Contents

*In Memory of Herman A. P. Schmidt, S.J.*

# Preface

This work may run the risk of appearing anachronistic, for who wishes to delve into Tridentine debates when more urgent matters are at hand? However, it is my impression that development in Roman Catholic theology and celebration of the eucharist, as well as the possibility of developing a fuller ecumenical communion at the Lord's Table, are both blocked by the difficulties which we experience in coming to grips with what happened at Trent, with what was taught there, and with why it was taught.

To studies of the Council of Trent, in historical context, we could apply the words of Pope John Paul II on the study of Martin Luther, written on the occasion of the reformer's 500th anniversary:

> ... it is necessary to continue an accurate historical work. By means of an investigation without preconceived ideas, motivated solely by a search for the truth, one must arrive at a true image of the reformer, of the whole period of the Reformation, and of the persons involved in it. Fault, where it exists, must be recognized, wherever it may lie. Where controversy has beclouded one's view, that view must be corrected independently of either party. Besides, we must not allow ourselves to be guided by the intention of setting ourselves up as judges of history, but solely by the motive of understanding better what happened and of becoming messengers of truth. Only by placing ourselves unreservedly in an attitude of purification by means of the truth can we find a shared interpretation of the past and at the same time reach a new point of departure for the dialogue of today' (Letter to Cardinal Jan Willebrands, *Origins* 13 (1983) 496).

David Noel Power, O.M.I.
*The Catholic University of America*
*Washington, D.C.*
*The First Sunday of Lenten Scrutinies 1985.*

# Acknowledgements

Passages from the following appear by kind permission of their publishers:

Anglican–Roman Catholic International Commission, *The Final Report* (London: SPCK 1982);

Concilium Tridentinum: *Diariorum, Actorum, Epistularum, Tractatuum Nova Collectio*, edited by the Societas Goerresiana (Freiburg im Breisgau: Herder & Co. 1901– ) vols. VI/1, VI/2, VII/1, VII/2, VIII;

Faith and Order Paper No. III, *Baptism, Eucharist and Ministry* (Geneva: World Council of Churches 1982);

Lutheran/Roman Catholic Joint Commission, *The Eucharist* (Geneva: The Lutheran World Federation 1980).

# Introduction

In its canons on the sacrifice of the Mass, the Council of Trent defined that the eucharist is not merely a commemoration of the sacrifice of the cross, nor only a sacrifice of praise and thanksgiving, but is itself a propitiatory sacrifice.[1] It was clearly referring to the ministerial act of the ordained priest in making this definition, as has been recently reaffirmed by the Roman Congregation for the Doctrine of the Faith. In commenting upon the *Final Report* of the ecumenical dialogue between the Anglican and Roman Catholic churches, this congregation questions the report's reading of the christian tradition on eucharistic sacrifice. It recalls the Catholic *dogma* in words that can be summarized as follows: the propitiatory value of the sacrifice of the mass is precisely the sacramental efficacy that arises from the fact that the church participates in the sacrificial act of the Lord through the ministry of the priest who, *in persona Christi*, repeats the words of the Lord at the Last Supper.[2]

On the other hand, in ecumenical dialogues and agreed statements there has been an attempt to express the doctrine on eucharistic sacrifice in other ways. Thus, in the Lima document of the Faith and Order Commission of the World Council of Churches, *Baptism, Eucharist and Ministry*, one reads this statement:

> It is in the light of the significance of the eucharist as intercession that reference to the eucharist in Catholic theology as 'propitiatory sacrifice' may be understood[3].

---

[1] The Council of Trent, Session XXII, canons 1 and 3: DS 1751, 1753.

[2] Congregation for the Doctrine of the Faith (CDF), 'Observations on the Final Report of ARCIC', *The Tablet* 236 (1982) 493.

[3] Faith and Order Paper No. 111, *Baptism, Eucharist and Ministry* (Geneva: WCC 1982). See the section on the Eucharist, Commentary no. 8, p. 11.

The reader of these words feels a little like Sarah laughing inside the tent, as she hears the Lord explaining to Abraham the meaning and consequences of the covenant. The reference to Catholic *theology* rather than to Catholic *dogma* is a neat turn of phrase, and the words *may be* are delightfully open to several readings, suggestive either of accepted interpretation or of freedom of interpretation, as the reader wishes.

These two typically different ways of adverting to the teaching of the Council of Trent in current discussions between churches raise the issue of how deep doctrinal agreement may be, and put a question to catholics as to how they are to understand and receive Trent's teaching.

There are also practical difficulties, affecting particularly the role of the priest in the celebration of the eucharist. Though the revision of liturgical books, in the light of early christian traditions, has brought churches closer to one another in the way that they celebrate, the Catholic Church still approves, and even promotes, certain practices that appear strange, if not erroneous, to other christians. Thus, for example, the revised Code of Canon Law supports and sanctions the practices of private mass and of offering mass stipends,[4] even while other churches raise questions about such practices, because of what they imply concerning the meaning of the eucharist.

This present work arises from the suspicion, voiced by Alasdair Heron, that 'the issue the Reformers addressed remains living still, at this point where the Roman Catholic conception of priesthood intersects with eucharistic theology in the doctrine of the sacrifice of the Mass'.[5] The study is undertaken, not to harden the differences, but to ask, from a Roman Catholic point of view, what may be implied today in a

---

[4] *Codex Iuris Canonici*, canons 945–958, 'De Oblata Ad Missae Celebrationem Stipe' and canon 904 on celebration 'individuali modo'.

[5] Alasdair I. C. Heron, *Table and Tradition: Toward an Ecumenical Understanding of the Eucharist* (Philadelphia: The Westminster Press 1983) 174.

reinterpretation of that part of our tradition. This, however, cannot be done without clear knowledge of what was exactly intended in the teaching of the Council of Trent. Hence, in a first chapter I will survey the position on sacrifice in recent agreed statements on the eucharist and in Rome's teaching. Then, in three chapters, I will investigate the teaching of the Council. In a further chapter, I will offer an interpretation of Trent and a way of re-reception which might open new avenues of dialogue, touching both doctrine and practice. Indeed, it is the inevitable inseparability of doctrine and practice which inspires the work.

Many another study on Trent's teaching on the eucharist is possible. One could look at the way in which the theologians and bishops used the scriptures or quoted patristic texts. One could consider the influence of the Pseudo-Dionysius, given the authority afforded this writer at that time. One could investigate the influence of important apologists like Gropper, Tapper or Cano, and see their conciliar interventions in the context of their writings. A study relating the debates on the real presence to those on sacrifice would also be useful. In this book, I have chosen to concentrate on one particular issue, which seems to be of importance today in ecumenical discussion and in liturgical change within the catholic church. In doing so, I have tried to isolate the main point of argument, to suggest a way of seeing it in its proper historical context, and to raise the issue of the reception of dogma in a way that might enable us to get beyond the impasse of artificial readings of the past.

# Chapter 1

# EUCHARISTIC SACRIFICE IN ECUMENICAL DIALOGUE

The interest of this work is in ecumenical dialogue that directly involves the Roman Catholic Church, especially through the agency of the Vatican Secretariate for Promoting Christian Unity. Several recent proposals for agreement on eucharistic doctrine and practice have come from dialogues in which this secretariate is a direct partner. Besides taking account of these, one also has to consider the proposal made at Lima by the Faith and Order Commission of the World Council of Churches, since the workings of this body involve official participation of theologians delegated by the Secretariate. It is impossible, however, to consider Catholic participation in ecumenical conversation without taking note of recent magisterial teaching on the eucharist, especially that of the Pope and of Roman dicasteries. Hence, this chapter will contain a survey of both ecumenical statements and magisterial teaching, as these touch on the sacrificial nature of the eucharist.

## I. Ecumenical Statements

The position of proposals for ecumenical agreement will be examined under several headings, in an attempt to synthesize the current approaches, rather than to look at each statement on its own. First of all, it will be seen how statements relate to the traditional catholic terminology about the sacrifice of the mass. Then, a look will be taken at explicit references to the teaching of the Council of Trent. Thirdly, it will be seen how the context of memorial is seen as the proper context in which to look at questions of sacrifice. Fourthly, some of the explanations of the tradition preferred by catholics or by others will be presented. Fifthly, note will be taken of how the proposals relate views on sacrifice to the role in the celebration of the eucharistic prayer. Sixthly, the place in the celebration allotted to ordained ministers will be examined.

## The Sacrifice of the Mass

Within the context of controversy, the term itself was a point of dissent at the time of the Reformation. Though other churches seem more tolerant today of catholic use of the term, they prefer not to adopt it themselves.

The agreed statement of the Roman Catholic/Lutheran World Federation records that Evangelical Lutherans still prefer 'to avoid even today any mention of "sacrifice of the Mass"' because of the way in which this very term seemed at an earlier age to support an autonomous sacrificial power for the priest (*eine selbstmächtige Opferkraft*), which undermined the part of the faithful in the sacrament and their reception of communion.[1] Elsewhere in this same statement it is recorded that Lutherans continue to experience difficulties with the catholic tradition of individual priestly celebration.[2]

In the Denver Report on the conversations between the Vatican Secretariate and the Methodist church, it is remarked that while Roman Catholics call the eucharist a sacrifice, Methodists prefer not to use this term.[3] This was in 1971. In the

[1] Lutheran/Roman Catholic Joint Commission, *The Eucharist* (Geneva: The Lutheran World Federation 1980) p. 21, n. 59. This will be referred to as *Eucharist*.

[2] ibid., p. 27, n. 76.

[3] 'Methodist-Roman Catholic Conversations: Denver Report', in *Growth in Agreement: Reports and Agreed Statements of Ecumenical Conversations on a World Level*, edited by Harding Meyer and Lukas Vischer (New York: Paulist, and Geneva: WCC 1984) p. 326, n. 83, II, 3. This volume will be referred to as *Growth*.

Dublin Report on these conversations in 1976, it is noted that Roman Catholics 'are accustomed to speak of the sacrifice of the Mass as something which the church offers in all ages of her history', as a making present of the sacrifice of the Cross, but that 'for some Methodists such language would imply that Christ is still being sacrificed'.[4]

Other ecumenical proposals show a scrupulous avoidance of the term 'sacrifice of the mass'.

## The Teaching of the Council of Trent

Even when it is not explicitly mentioned, it is always clear that the formulation of catholic teaching by the Council of Trent is at issue in ecumenical dialogue on the eucharist. Hence, it is all the more interesting to see what is done with it when it is explicitly mentioned.

The ARCIC (Anglican Roman Catholic International Commission) Report makes but a passing reference to Trent, where it notes the Council's use of *commemoratio* and *repraesentatio* in relating the eucharist to the cross.[5] The Lima statement of the Faith and Order Commission of the World Council of Churches asks for a reconsideration of the question of sacrifice in the light of sixteenth century controversies, and offers the explanation that catholic theology on the propitiatory nature of the sacrifice is to be related to the practice of intercession in the celebration of the eucharist.[6] This is indeed a suggestion that raises eyebrows, if it is meant to be a way of explaining Trent.

The document that gives most attention to the teaching of Trent is the agreed statement reached by the delegates of the

[4] *Growth*, p. 354, n. 66.

[5] Anglican-Roman Catholic International Commission, *The Final Report* (London: SPCK 1982), p. 19, n. 5. This will be referred to as ARCIC.

[6] Faith and Order Paper No. 111, *Baptism, Eucharist and Ministry* (Geneva: WCC 1982), commentary no. 8, p. 11. This will be referred to as *Lima*.

Vatican Secretariate and those of the World Lutheran Federation. This statement adopted the interesting method of stating first the points of doctrine on which both churches could be invited to agree, and then stating those issues on which some disagreement was felt to persist. In stating those issues, it presents first the Roman Catholic position and then the Lutheran. Some appendices to the document treat of controversial issues, in the light of proposed agreement and continuing problems.

All of this material is to be found in a booklet published in 1978 entitled *Das Herrenmahl*, and then in English in 1980, entitled *The Eucharist*, rather than *The Lord's Supper*.[7] In presenting the catholic position on the sacrifice of the mass, the document quotes the definition of Trent that it is a sacrifice of propitiation, along with the teaching from the decree's chapter that in this sacrifice victim and offerer are the same as on the cross, only the manner of offering being different. It also quotes the canon which says that the sacrifice can be offered for the living and the dead, for sins, punishments, satisfactions and other necessities.[8] To give a contemporary reading of these teachings, the catholic partners to the dialogue make four points. First of all, they explain that those who participate in the eucharist are able to share in Christ's self-offering.[9] Secondly, they follow this statement with the idea that, having nothing else to offer, christians can offer Christ himself to God.[10] This is intended to meet the difficulty that the mass may seem to add something to the sacrifice of the cross, but it is an interesting way around the problem, since one does not find in Trent the

[7] The German edition of this document is: Gemeinsame Römisch-Katholische/Evangelisch-Lutheranische Kommission, *Das Herrenmahl* (Paderborn: Bonifacius 1978). An earlier English edition, without appendices, had appeared in *Origins* 8 (1979) 465–478.

[8] *Eucharist* p. 20, n. 57.

[9] ibid., pp. 20f, n. 58.

[10] l.c.

statement that the church offers Christ, or that christians offer Christ, even though it is said that the victim offered is Christ, or that Christ is the priest acting through the ordained minister.

A third point that is pertinent to an understanding of Trent is made in another section of the document, where the catholic partners recall the catholic tradition of making intercession for the dead.[11] A fourth point is closely connected to this, namely, the teaching that the efficaciousness of the fruits of the mass transcends the immediate circle of those who gather together to celebrate it.[12]

On the evangelical side, in counterposition to catholic explanations, the Lutherans recall the problems arising at the time of the Reformation concerning the power of the priest and the exclusion of the faithful.[13] In keeping with this, they elsewhere express their views about the undesirability of private or individual celebration of the eucharist by ordained priests.[14] They likewise recall the polemic at the time of the Reformation against ideas of *ex opere operato* efficacy of the mass's offering and give this as a reason for which they prefer not to use the term 'sacrifice of the mass'.[15]

The position on *ex opere operato* efficacy is treated at some length in an appendix to the document, written by a catholic, Vinzenz Pfnür.[16] Pfnür attributes the Reformers' difficulties with the *ex opere operato* efficacy of catholic teaching almost wholly to an impoverished theology of the fruits of the mass, connected with the names of Scotus and Biel, and to exaggerated practices of popular devotion, such as those which attributed added value to the mass when a number of masses

[11] *Eucharist* p. 25, n. 70.
[12] ibid., p. 22, n. 61(d).
[13] ibid., p. 21, n. 59.
[14] ibid., p. 23, n. 63.
[15] ibid., p. 21, n. 59.
[16] ibid., p. 76–80.

were celebrated in an unbroken series, or when mass was offered in honour of a saint, or with a certain number of lighted candles on the altar, or an extended number of orations, and the like. He notes that Luther and the other Reformers seem to have paid little attention to catholic theologians who stressed the relation of the mass to the cross and encouraged the communion of the faithful, or to catholic attempts at the reform of practice. In explaining the matter in this way, he is following a position made popular by writers such as Lortz and Iserloh.[17] He then concludes as follows:

> Contextually, then, there is now a convergence inasmuch as the Catholic side, vis-à-vis a ritualistic exteriorization and the concept of the Mass as a work *ex opere operato* . . . stresses the importance of the participation in faith of the whole of the celebrating congregation and, further, inasmuch as vis-à-vis the concept of the *ex opere operato* finite value of the Mass in contrast with the sacrifice of the Cross the same side teaches the unity of the Mass and sacrifice of the Cross . . . while the popular view of the unfailing effect of certain forms of Mass and Mass series for the redemption of a soul was already corrected by the Council of Trent; on the other side, there is a convergence inasmuch as the Lutheran side, vis-à-vis an individualistic understanding of the Lord's Supper as a granting of the remission of sins of an individual, places greater emphasis on the community of the body of Christ and does not reject the possibility of a supplication for the dead.[18]

In these references to the teaching of Trent, in brief, we see a catholic tendency to explain Reformation difficulties in terms of misunderstandings engendered by popular practice and a particular medieval theology about the fruits of the mass, which supported this practice, at least in part. Along with this historical

---

[17] Pfnür refers to the work of Iserloh on p. 78, note 10. More will be said of this in the next chapter.

[18] ibid., p. 79.

explanation, there goes a reflection on the mass as sacrifice which takes up the ideas of the church's self-offering in offering Christ and of prayer for the dead. On the other hand, on the Lutheran side there remains the possibility that a practice which highlights the ministerial priesthood would not be acceptable, and consequently a question-mark against any doctrinal position that goes along with such a practice. Both the Lutheran/Roman Catholic dialogue and the passing reference of the Lima document to propitiatory sacrifice suggest that there is more to be said about this issue before full and clear agreement is reached between catholics and other christian churches.

## Memorial as Context

A common feature of dialogical statements is that they have resorted to the jewish practice and notion of memorial, both as a central category for eucharistic theology and as a particular way whereby to address the issue of sacrifice, which allows one to relate the eucharist to the cross. In the documents under survey, the greek word *anamnesis* is often used, summoning to the mind the supper narrative in the New Testament, as well as the liturgies and writings of the early church.

In using the idea of memorial or *anamnesis*, the attempt is to give an integral and biblical theology of the eucharist, rooted in eucharistic practice, which does not separate sacrament from sacrifice, so that one can talk of the eucharist as a sacramental sacrifice, commemorating and representing the one unrepeatable offering of Christ on the cross. In none of the documents in question is there any possibility of referring to an offering made in the mass over and above the one offering of Christ. Whatever offering is made in the eucharist is a renewal in sacramental form of Christ's offering. On this foundation, one can note some differences in approach in the various statements, differences that indicate that despite the common use of *anamnesis* there is as yet no firm theological understanding of the term and of its implications.

The Lima statement makes memorial central to its presentation of eucharistic doctrine and to its suggestions about practice. It can thus include under this heading whatever is to be said about sacrifice. However, from the outset one notices that the document is not thoroughly consistent in what it says of the object of memorial, or in its use of the word *sacrifice*. It can, for example, juxtapose these two affirmations:

> The eucharist is the memorial of the crucified and risen Christ, i.e. the living and effective sign of his sacrifice, accomplished once and for all on the cross and still operative on behalf of all humankind.[19]

and

> Christ himself with all that he has accomplished for us and for all creation (in his incarnation, servanthood, ministry, teaching, suffering, sacrifice, resurrection, ascension and sending of the Spirit) is present in this *anamnesis*, granting us communion with himself. . . .[20]

In comparing these two statements, we see that in the first what is said to be remembered is the sacrifice of the cross, whereas in the second it is stated that the sacrifice is remembered and made present along with much else that is pertinent to the reality of humanity's redemption through the Saviour. The first affirmation is closer to sixteenth century perspectives, when a theology of redemption concentrated almost exclusively on Christ's death, whereas the second affirmation is more in keeping with patristic and liturgical traditions, which are more extensive in their remembering. What has to be queried is

[19] *Lima*, p. 11, n. 5.
[20] ibid., n. 6.

Lima's apparent restriction of sacrifice to Christ's death, since this has implications both for an understanding of redemption and for eucharistic prayer.

One finds similar ambiguities in the ARCIC Final Report. In one and the same paragraph that report can state on the one hand that Christ's death was his sacrifice and on the other hand that sacrificial language in the New Testament refers to the historical events of 'Christ's saving work for us', apparently allowing for a broader inclusion of the mysteries of his flesh.[21] The statements of the Lutheran/Roman Catholic and of the Reformed/Roman Catholic dialogues restrict the usage of the word *sacrifice* to the death of Christ,[22] and the Roman Catholic/Methodist proposal speaks in a somewhat more inclusive way of the 'triumphant sacrifice' of his death.[23]

As far as the word *anamnesis* or memorial is concerned, all the statements credit it with meaning some kind or another of efficacious representation of what is remembered. Thus the Lima statement affirms:

> The eucharist is the memorial of the crucified and risen Christ, i.e. the living and effective sign of his sacrifice, accomplished once and for all on the cross and still operative on behalf of all humankind. The biblical idea of memorial as applied to the eucharist refers to this present efficacy of God's work when it is celebrated by God's people in liturgy.[24]

Further on, the same document states:

> The anamnesis in which Christ acts through the joyful celebration of his Church is thus both representation and anticipation. It is not only a calling to mind of what is past and of

[21] ARCIC, p. 13, n. 5 & p. 20, n. 5.
[22] *Eucharist*, p. 19, n. 56.
[23] *Growth*, p. 326, n. 2.
[24] *Lima*, p. 11, n. 5.

its significance. It is the Church's effective proclamation of God's mighty acts and promises.[25]

The ARCIC Final Report in explaining why the eucharist has been called a sacrifice uses a comparable understanding of anamnesis:

> The tradition of the Church, as evidenced for example in its liturgies, used (sacrificial) language to designate in the eucharistic celebration the *anamnesis* of this historical event. Therefore it is possible to say at the same time that there is only one unrepeatable sacrifice in the historical sense, but that the eucharist is a sacrifice in the sacramental sense, provided that it is clear that this is not a repetition of the historical sacrifice.[26]

This is an extremely foreshortened explanation of how sacrificial language was introduced into liturgies, and could not be pressed very far for historical accuracy, but the intention of relating eucharist to the cross by way of efficacious sacramental representation is clear. Similar ideas of efficacious representation are to be found in this assertion of the Roman Catholic/Lutheran dialogue:

> In the memorial celebration of the people of God more happens than that past events are brought to mind by the power of recall and imagination. The decisive point is not that what is past is called to mind, but that the Lord calls his people into his presence and confronts them with his salvation. In this creative act of God, the salvific event from the past becomes the offer of salvation for the present and the promise of salvation for the future.[27]

The strongly Lutheran emphasis in this statement on the

[25] ibid., n. 7.
[26] ARCIC, p. 20, n. 5.
[27] *Eucharist*, p. 13, n. 36.

Lord's offer of salvation, or on the Lord's call, is a reminder that while the rhetoric of efficacious memorial may be now widely accepted, its further explanation is not easy. The ecumenical documents here under consideration seem to follow two distinct avenues in providing this explanation, one which concentrates on the church's self-offering with Christ, the other on the efficacious working of the eucharistic prayer, or sacrifice of praise.

## Christ's Offering and the Church's Offering

It was noted above that the Lima statement sees more than the representation of Christ's sacrificial death in the eucharistic memorial, including as it does the remembrance of the whole saving activity of the Lord. However, when it comes to an understanding of the sacrificial meaning of the eucharist all the statements concentrate on the representation of the Lord's death, in and through which he offered himself to the Father. As the Reformed/Roman Catholic dialogue puts it,

> In its joyful prayer of thanksgiving, 'in the Eucharist', when the Church of Christ remembers his reconciling death for our sins and for the sins of the whole world, Christ himself is present, who 'gave himself up on our behalf as an offering and sacrifice whose fragrance is pleasing to God' (Eph 5.2).[28]

This understanding of the sacramental representation or re-enactment of Christ's own self-offering provides a foundation for the church's self-offering, which is made in Christ and in communion with his offering. Thus the above quoted paragraph continues:

> Sanctified by his Spirit, the Church, through, with, and in God's Son, Jesus Christ, offers itself to the Father. It thereby becomes a living sacrifice of thanksgiving.[29]

[28] 'Reformed-Roman Catholic Conversations', in *Growth*, p. 452, n. 81.
[29] l.c.

This seems to be the explanation of the sacrificial nature of the eucharist preferred by Roman Catholic participants in most of these dialogues. This is particularly obvious in the Roman Catholic/Lutheran dialogues, where Trent itself is interpreted in these terms. It would seem that this linkage between a sacramental representation of Christ's self-offering and the church's self-offering allows catholics to give substance to a long-standing tradition of strongly sacrificial language, according to which the church offers sacrifice to God, without derogating from the once-for-all sufficiency of Christ's death. As the Methodist/Roman Catholic statement says, Roman Catholics 'are accustomed to speak of the sacrifice of the Mass as something which the church offers in all ages of her history'.[30] Indeed, the Catholic party to the Lutheran/Roman Catholic dialogue absorbs the church's self-offering into Christ's self-offering, so that it is in offering him (as Trent says, the only victim in the eucharistic sacrifice) that the church offers itself:

> The members of the body of Christ are united through Christ with God and with one another in such a way that they become participants in his worship, his self-offering, his sacrifice to the Father. Through this union between Christ and Christians, the eucharistic assembly 'offers Christ' by consenting in the power of the Holy Spirit to be offered by him to the Father. Apart from Christ, we have no gifts, no worship, no sacrifice of our own to offer to God. All we can plead is Christ, the sacrificial lamb and victim whom the Father himself has given us.[31]

The Lutheran party to the dialogue, however, does not seem to have been very enthusiastic about this kind of language, simply preferring, as already noted, not to speak at all of the sacrifice of the Mass. This is not to say that they did not see room in the Lord's Supper for the self-offering of the faithful, since

[30] *Growth*, p. 354, n. 66.
[31] *Eucharist*, pp. 20f., n. 58.

they had only to recall Luther's own words 'that we offer with Christ, that is ... we cast ourselves upon Christ with unwavering faith in his testament and we do not appear otherwise before God with our prayer, praise and sacrifice than through Him'.[32] However, for them, this self-offering in Christ, or any kind of offering of Christ even as the Catholic party had explained it, was hardly to be made the central point of eucharistic theology.

In face of the catholic predilection for the language of offering, and for an inclusion of self-offering in Christ at the heart of the mystery, the Methodists also retained a great reserve, noting that 'such language would imply that Christ is still being sacrificed'.[33] Hence they offered their own understanding in these words:

> Methodists prefer to say that Christ has offered one sacrifice for sins and now lives to make intercession for us, so that we in union with him can offer ourselves to the Father, making his sacrificial death our only plea.[34]

While the Faith and Order Lima statement preserves traditional references to the church's self-offering in the eucharist, it does so with considerable reserve, perhaps relating it more to communion than to any other aspect of the celebration:

> In Christ we offer ourselves as a living and holy sacrifice in our daily lives (Rom. 12.1; I Peter 2.5); this spiritual worship, acceptable to God, is nourished in the eucharist, in which we are sanctified and reconciled in love, in order to be servants of reconciliation in the world.[35]

[32] ibid., p. 21, n. 60.
[33] *Growth*, p. 354, n. 66.
[34] ibid.
[35] *Lima*, p. 12, n. 10.

The ARCIC report is somewhat vague on this score, but it seems to make a distinction between the representation of Christ's sacrifice in the repetition by the priest of the Lord's words at the Supper, and the church's self-offering which is done through the priest in the eucharistic prayer.[36] This is to connect the church's self-offering with the efficacious representation of Christ's death, but to avoid making the self-offering of Christ in any way intrinsic to an act of offering made by the church, or to make the church's own self-offering intrinsic to Christ's sacramental offering of himself as head of the body.

It is none too clear, however, that this is ARCIC's position, for whereas in one place we read,

> Because the eucharist is the memorial of the sacrifice of Christ, the action of the presiding minister in reciting again the words of Christ at the last supper and distributing to the assembly the holy gifts is seen to stand in a sacramental relation to what Christ himself did in offering his own sacrifice,[37]

in another we read,

> In the celebration of the memorial, Christ in the Holy Spirit unites his people with himself in a sacramental way so that the Church enters into the movement of his self-offering,[38]

and

> In the eucharistic prayer the church continues to make a perpetual memorial of Christ's death, and his members, united with God and with one another, give thanks for all his mercies, entreat the benefits of his passion on behalf of the whole church,

[36] ARCIC, p. 41, n. 2 & p. 14, n. 5.
[37] ibid., p. 35, n. 13. Compare p. 41, n. 2.
[38] ibid., p. 20, n. 5.

participate in these benefits and enter into the movement of his self-offering.[39]

This may be simply a case of a failure to coordinate the right and the left hand, but it is linked to two distinct theological issues, with which the ARCIC report appears to have trouble. The one is the place of the eucharistic prayer in the efficacious representation of Christ's death, the other the role of the priest in the sacramental sacrifice. Let us look at how these issues appear in the whole set of ecumenical statements.

*Sacramental Sacrifice and Eucharistic Prayer*
In brief, the preferred catholic explanation of sacrificial language in these statements seems to consist in relating a self-offering by the church to the sacramental representation of Christ's sacrifice, so that the church can be said either to offer itself along with Christ, or even indeed to offer Christ. This explanation appears to be substantially acceptable to those of the protestant and reformed traditions, even though they continue to have problems with the terms or perhaps to feel that the explanation does not address all problems, especially those affecting the role of the ordained minister. Before, however, looking at this, we can see how the sacramental memorial and the eucharistic prayer are connected in the statements, this being pertinent to how the role of the priest is seen, in its twofold relationship to Christ and to the church.

As far as the ARCIC report is concerned, we have just seen how on the one hand it places the sacramental representation of Christ's sacrifice in the eucharistic prayer, but on the other places it in the priest's repetition of the words of Christ at the Supper. The second explanation either isolates the action of the priest from the act of the community at this point, or it isolates

[39] ibid., p. 14, n. 5.

the words of Jesus from the prayer, making of them the essential proclamation through which the Lord's death is sacramentally represented as offer of salvation for the church. The first meaning would be more in line with a traditional catholic emphasis on the sacramentality of the priest, the second with a traditional protestant emphasis on the testamentary and proclamatory nature of Christ's words.

The Faith and Order Commission, on the other hand, in its Lima statement has no hesitation in attributing representation and anticipation to the prayer of thanksgiving and intercession,[40] while at the same time noting how 'the words and acts of Christ at the institution of the eucharist stand at the heart of the celebration'.[41] This is but to recall that the efficacious representation and anticipation of the Lord's saving work within the sacrament, and expressed in the eucharistic prayer, has to be done in memory of Christ and in conjunction with the recall and proclamation of his words.

The Lutheran/Roman Catholic statement, for its part, does not directly attribute sacramental power to the eucharistic prayer, but states that the sacrifice of praise offered in this prayer is dependent on the sacrifice of the cross and that thanksgiving for this sacrifice is its primary content. The statement speaks for both traditions in this paragraph:

> Our two traditions agree in understanding the Eucharist as a sacrifice of praise. This is neither simple verbal praise, nor is it a supplement or a complement which people from their own power add to the offering of praise and thanksgiving which Christ has made to the Father. The eucharistic sacrifice of praise has only become possible through the sacrifice of Christ on the cross: therefore this remains the main content of the church's sacrifice of praise. Only 'by him, with him, and in him who is our great High Priest and Intercessor we offer to the Father, in

[40] *Lima*, p. 11, n. 8.
[41] ibid., p. 12, n. 13.

the power of the Holy Spirit, our praise, thanksgiving and intercession'.[42]

Methodists, in their dialogue with Roman Catholics, admit the legitimacy of talking of a sacrifice of praise and thanksgiving, along with the self-offering of the church and the pleading of Christ's offering here and now, but they establish no connection between these different things. The World Alliance of Reformed Churches and the Catholic delegates in their conversation could, on the other hand, agree on this statement about the efficacy of the prayer:

> In its joyful prayer of thanksgiving, in the eucharist, when the Church of Christ remembers his reconciling death for our sins and for the sins of the whole world, Christ himself is present, who etc. (see the quotation of this statement already given above).

## The Role of the Priest

From what has already been said, it would seem that the ARCIC report makes an effective distinction between the sacramental relationship of the priest to Christ in the recitation of the Lord's words and the distribution of the gifts to the people[43] and his relationship to the church when, in presiding at the eucharist and proclaiming the prayer, he is 'representative of the whole Church in the fulfilment of its priestly vocation of self-offering to God as a living sacrifice'.[44] In one respect, this sounds very like the teaching of Pius XII in *Mediator Dei* on the role of the priest, where representation of the church is made subordinate to the priest's representation of Christ,[45] but the

---

[42] *Eucharist*, p. 13, n. 37. See also pp. 8f., nn. 21–24 on the Holy Spirit.
[43] See above, notes 36 & 37.
[44] ARCIC, p. 36, n. 13.
[45] Pius XII, *Mediator Dei*, DS 3850–3853.

Congregation on the Doctrine of the Faith was dissatisfied with ARCIC, probably because it does not clearly enough say that in his sacramental relationship to Christ the priest renews the sacrificial oblation of Christ.

This, of course, is an element in catholic tradition which raises problems for all protestant churches. We already saw how the Lutherans, in face of the catholic interpretation of Trent recall the Reformers' difficulties over the power attributed to priests and the accompanying practices of offering for the living and the dead and of celebrating private masses. For the authors of the Lutheran/Roman Catholic statement, there is no disagreement between the two parties on the traditional importance of having an ordained minister to preside over the Lord's Supper or eucharistic celebration. Difficulties arise for the Lutherans in what catholics think the priest can do by himself, and for catholics in the readiness of Lutherans to allow for the exceptional case when a eucharist may be celebrated without an ordained minister,[46] or more basically, with Lutheran orders themselves. The catholic position on the need for an ordained minister is stated as follows:

> ... The ordination of a bishop or a priest is ... the essential prerequisite to their presiding at the Lord's Supper: even in exceptional cases there can be no eucharistic celebration without an ordained priest. Insofar as the sacrament of ordination is lacking, the Catholic Church sees even separated Christians as not having 'preserved the genuine and total reality (*substantia*) of the eucharistic mystery'.[47]

The statement here quotes the Decree on Ecumenism of the Second Vatican Council,[48] which is already a modification of

---

[46] *Eucharist*, pp. 23f., n. 66.
[47] l.c.
[48] Vatican, Decree on Ecumenism, n. 22.

18

standard catholic theology on the validity of order, which simply considered whether or not the one saying the Lord's words had the power to consecrate and offer. On the other hand, there are echoes in the Decree of the Council of Trent's reluctance in canon 7 of its decree on the sacrament of order to dismiss the ordinations of the Reformers as invalid, simply dismissing them as illegitimate.[49] The Vatican Council seemed to recognize that catholic positions had hardened since Trent, and that the issues of eucharistic reality could not be reduced to the power of the minister through succession in order. When one takes the eucharist as a gift of the Lord to the church and an assembly of the church in the communion of faith and remembrance, the role of the presider has to be considered in this context and not only in terms of the power conferred upon him in order. For this reason, the Decree on Ecumenism, to which the dialogue refers, used the nuanced expression about the 'genuine and total reality'.

The Faith and Order Commission of the WCC in its Lima document explains the role of the minister as that of presider, combining this with the idea that it is the Lord himself who presides at the celebration through the minister:

> It is Christ who invites to the meal and presides at it . . . In most churches, this presidency is signified by an ordained minister. The one who presides at the eucharistic celebration in the name of Christ makes clear that the rite is not the assembly's own creation or possession; the eucharist is a gift from Christ living in his Church.[50]

According to this explanation, not only is the priest given his sacramental role in clear relation to the assembly, but the Lord's own sacramental action is presented as something which he does

[49] DS 1777.
[50] *Lima*, p. 16, n. 29.

in and through the church gathered in assembly. This makes it impertinent to think of the minister's action as something in which the people participate, or as something which he could perform on his own. The representation of Christ takes on meaning only within the context of the church's celebration in the assembly of faith.

## Conclusion

The considerations on memorial, eucharistic prayer, and ordained ministry, that emerge in these ecumenical agreements on the eucharist, show a new context in which the teaching of the Council of Trent on the mass as propitiatory sacrifice is considered, either implicitly or explicitly. By effectively placing this tradition in a new doctrinal and ecclesial context, the dialogues make it necessary to reconsider Trent's emphasis on the act of the ordained priest and on the power of the priest to offer the mass for the living and the dead. At the same time, there is no uniform position in the documents examined as to how the efficacious representation of Christ's sacrifice comes about, or as to how the thanksgiving and self-offering of the church are to be related to this sacramental sacrifice. Still less is there a clear position on the role of the ordained minister. One is left with the impression that, however much agreement emerges on the relation of the eucharist to the cross, it is difficult for catholics in these dialogues to incorporate Trent's emphasis on the sacramental role of the priest in offering the mass, or the traditional catholic practice of having the mass offered for the living and the dead. Even though we have not yet examined what Trent understood by this practice, we can already register the suspicion that its ideas about the propitiatory sacrifice cannot be reduced to intercession for the living and the dead, nor explained simply by the intercession made for the dead in pleading the sacrifice of Christ within the eucharistic prayer. There is a connection between the offering of the mass for the living and the dead and what Trent understood of the power of the priest, and this issue does have to be squarely faced, granted that this can be done in a new context, where some of the implications of making memorial are better understood than they were in the sixteenth century because of a revival in biblical studies. In any case, it is the role of the priest in the eucharist which emerges as one of the primary concerns in the Roman Catholic magisterium.

## II. The Contemporary Roman Magisterium

In its response to the Final Report of the ARCIC Commission, the Roman Congregation on the Doctrine of the Faith indicated reservations on its positions on sacrifice and ministry, the two being interconnected. It cited the teaching of John Paul II in a letter of 1980 on the eucharistic mystery in making its comments. In this magisterial teaching, explicit reference is made to the teaching of the Council of Trent on the sacrifice of the mass. Following the inspiration of the Second Vatican Council, Congregation and Pope do indeed treat the eucharist as a mystery of the church and explore the active participation of the faithful in its celebration, particularly through eucharistic communion. However, they both clearly wish to retrieve the teaching on priesthood and its connection to sacrifice in terms that are drawn from Trent.

Pope John Paul writes of the eucharist as the sacramental representation of Christ's sacrifice of propitiation.[51] The word *propitiation* alternates with *redemption* and *restitution*, depending on the aspect of Christ's sacrifice that the pope wishes to accentuate. Thus while *restitution* suggests restoration and

[51] John Paul II, 'Dominicae Cenae: Epistula de SS. Eucharistiae Mysterio et Cultu' *Notitiae* XVI (1980) 138, n. 8 & 139–142, n. 9. The complete text is to be found pp. 125–154. This will be referred to as DC.

rebuilding of what has been lost by sin, the word *propitiation* more directly indicates that this sacrifice was made for sin and for sinners. While the language of commemoration and representation is used to relate the eucharist to the cross, the primary category of understanding that the pope uses in a theology of eucharist is that of *sacrifice*. Thus, communion in the body and blood of Christ is described as a participation in the fruits of the sacrifice,[52] even while the aspect of fraternal community is being put forward. The accent on the need to offer this sacrifice in order to make propitiation, and to enjoy the fruits of propitiation, is highlighted when the pope reminds the faithful that they should approach it with reverence and even caution, and not without a frequent use of the sacrament of penance, and tells bishops that they should assure this frequency in the pastoral direction that they give to their churches.[53]

While the sacrifice of the eucharist, according to the letter, is the sacrifice of the church, it is confided in the first place to bishops and priests and is the primary exercise of their ministry.[54] The sacramental act or offering itself is constituted by the act of the priest when he consecrates and offers *in persona Christi*.[55] The sacramental relation of the priest to Christ in this act is that he is almost the same person as Christ, the eternal high priest.[56]

The letter then describes the active participation of the

[52] DC 131, n. 4: 'Nam Ecclesia ad effectum perducitur cum nos hac in fraterna communitate et consociatione sacrificium celebramus crucis Christi, cum annuntiamus mortem Domini donec veniat, ac postmodum cum, penitus mysterio salutis nostrae pervasi, accedimus communitaria ratione ad Domini mensam, ut modo sacramentali fructibus nutriamur Sancti Sacrificii propitiatorii.'

[53] DC 146, n. 11.

[54] DC 126–128, n. 2, under the heading *Eucharistia et Sacerdotium*.

[55] DC 137f., n. 8.

[56] ibid.: '... ratione peculiari et sacramentali idem prorsus sit ac summus aeternusque Sacerdos'.

congregation in the eucharist as a response to the words and actions of the priest, whereby the words and acts of Christ at the supper are represented.[57] In the same paragraph, it says that the priest is inserted sacramentally into the immolation of Christ's sacrifice, whereas the congregation shares in this spiritually.[58] The notion that the church shares in the self-offering of Christ through the eucharist, which has been seen to be part of the catholic position described in the catholic/lutheran dialogue, receives repeated mention in the magisterium of John Paul,[59] but in this letter we see that this is joined with a fundamental distinction between the sacramental offering of the priest and the spiritual offering of the congregation.

In repeating this teaching, the Congregation on the Doctrine of the Faith in a letter of August 1983 attributes more meaning to the expression *in persona Christi* than to *nomine Christi* or *Christi vicem (gerens)*.[60] The reaction of the same organisation to the position of ARCIC on ordained ministry and its role in the eucharist has already been recorded. These two documents of the congregation indicate that it wishes to single out the action of the priest in the eucharist as the sacramental act whereby Christ is present and acts, and that it follows John Paul II in accentuating the Tridentine doctrine of propitiation. Not only does it say this in reacting to the doctrine on ministry of the

[57] DC 137, n. 8: 'Verba uniuscuiusque sacerdotis et acta, quibus totius eucharisticae congregationis conscia actuosaque participatione respondet, referunt quasi vocis imagine dicta et facta Ultimae Cenae.'

[58] DC 138, n. 8: 'Conscientia autem huius rei aliquomodo illuminat significationem et indolem sacerdotis-celebrantis qui, Sanctissimum immolans Sacrificium atque in persona Christi agens, inducitur inseriturque modo sacramentali (simulque ineffabili) in hoc intimum sacrum ubi is vicissim spiritaliter omnes consociat eucharisticae congregationis participes.'

[59] Cf., for example, 'Discours des Audiences Générales: l'eucharistie comme sacrifice et le repas eucharistique', *Documentation Catholique* LXXX (1983) 673f.

[60] Congregation for the Doctrine of the Faith, 'Epistula de Ministro Eucharistiae AAS LXXV (1983) 1006.

ARCIC report, but it makes its point even more clearly in reference to the use made of *anamnesis* in this report. The congregation in its observations on the report queries what is meant by the effectual proclamation, whereby the once-for-all event of the passion becomes operative in the present. It recalls the catholic *dogma* of propitiatory sacrifice: 'the propitiatory value that Catholic dogma attributes to the Eucharist ... is precisely that of this sacramental efficacy', that is to say, the participation of the church in the sacrificial act of the Lord, 'by the ministry of the priest saying *in persona Christi* the words of the Lord'.[61]

In as much as this Roman magisterial teaching highlights the nature of the mass as a sacrifice of propitiation, and in as much as it associates this belief with the sacramental action and words of the ordained priest, it offers another interpretation of Trent than that of the ecumenical documents already examined. There are ways, however, in which this magisterium may modify the Tridentine teaching.

The papal teaching does consider the eucharist as a mystery and act of the church and is more sensitive to the part that the congregation plays in the sacrifice than is the teaching of Trent. Thus, the pope always speaks of the sacrifice as one in which the church takes part as a community, and sees the strengthening of communion in the church as a fruit of the sacrifice and of a sharing in it by sacramental communion. He is also insistent on the whole congregation's share in the Lord's self-offering through active participation. Nothing is said in the letter *Dominicae Cenae* about private or solitary mass, in the strict sense of the term, though of course support for this occurs in other parts of Rome's teaching.

On the other hand, the papal teaching gives a very distinctive

---

[61] Congregation for the Doctrine of the Faith, 'Observations on the Final Report of ARCIC', *Tablet* 236 (1982) 493.

quality to the role of the priest in citing the Council of Trent, and identifies the priest very closely with the person of Jesus Christ in appealing to the Council. In distinguishing between the part of the priest and the part of the congregation in offering the sacrifice of the Lord, the pope uses a distinction which is found in the Tridentine decree on the mass in a way that may go beyond the Council's usage. In talking of the private mass in the technical sense of a mass celebrated with the faithful, but without their participation through communion, the decree states that this is a public act both because of the public nature of the priest's ministry and because of the spiritual communion of the people in the priest's sacramental act. John Paul in *Dominicae Cenae* makes a general principle of this distinction, so that even in those masses in which the faithful receive communion they are said to share in the offering spiritually, as distinct from the minister's sacramental participation. The idea behind this is that Christ's sacrifice is made sacramentally present through the priest and through the priest alone, so that the congregation may then share in it spiritually.

Of Trent, it will be noted that it chose general terms to treat of the way in which Christ acts through the priest, or offers through him, even while assuming that this is done through the words of the institution narrative. Its words are compatible with several theories, even probably with that which sees the priest to receive power from Christ to offer his sacrifice in the name of the church. John Paul, however, gives a strongly representative character to this relationship, even to the point of quasi-identification of the minister with Christ, the high-priest, and of making of his repetition of the supper words a kind of dramatization of the last supper. It is to this end that he employs the term *in persona Christi*, one that does not occur in the magisterial teaching of Trent. In that sense, for the papal teaching, and for the congregation which is its auxiliary, the priest is a presence of Christ in the celebration of the eucharist in a way that goes beyond dogma. Because of the way in which this contrasts with ecumenical approaches, it is important to examine what was that dogma.

## Chapter 2

# THE COUNCIL OF TRENT: BACKGROUND[1]

It was during its temporary location in the city of Bologna that the question of the sacrifice of the mass was first put before the Council, as an issue distinct from the sacrament of the eucharist. At Bologna, only the theologians called to the Council had time to give their views, but at Trent in 1551 and 1552 the matter was taken up by both theologians and Council Fathers. The discussion, however, was not brought to a close at that session, so that the decree was taken up again at the final synodal meeting of 1562.

The starting-point in 1547, and again in 1551, was provided by a list of articles, condensing the views of the Reformers (referred to as heretics), by way of objections to catholic belief and catholic practice found in their writings. Though there is some slight difference between the list of 1547 and that of 1551, the two can be considered together, in order to see how the leading figures of the Council understood the point of controversy.[2]

Though a number of those taking part in the Council probably knew nothing of the writings of the Reformers apart

[1] The full title of the edition of the Acts of the Council of Trent is: *Concilium Tridentinum: Diariorum, Actorum, Epistularum, Tractatuum Nova Collectio*, edited by the Societas Goerresiana and published by Herder & Co., Freiburg im Breisgau. The abbreviation CT will be used to refer to this collection, followed by the volume number and the page and line reference, e.g. CT VII/2 (tome 7, volume 2) 111 (page) 23 (line). A summary of the Council's doings on the sacrifice of the mass can be found in Hubert Jedin, *Geschichte des Konzils Von Trient* (Freiburg im Breisgau: Herder 1970/75 Band III 338–358, Band IV/I 174–209).

[2] For the articles presented at Bologna, cf. CT VI/1 322–323 4: for those presented at Trent in 1551, cf. CT VII/I 375–377 13.

from the lists of errors presented to them, one can nonetheless say that the knowledge of these writings possessed by the Council was quite good, though often presented in a biased way and with an apologetical rather than an irenic interest. Prior to the synodal gatherings, lists of errors from these writings had been prepared by Johannes Cochlaeus, Johannes Eck, Johannes Faber and Alphonsus de Castro, and these were used in drawing up articles for conciliar debate.[3] It is also clear from a number of interventions, particularly by theologians, that the speaker was well acquainted with some at least of the Reformation writings.

In considering the list of errors on the sacrifice of the mass presented at Bologna, one can also take account of a list prepared by Seripando.[4] This list is useful, not only because Seripando seems to have influenced the official list, but also because he gives explicit reference to the Reformers from whose works he excerpted the propositions, and the *Societas Goerresiana* in its editorial work has given exact annotations to the writings concerned. The official list of articles considered in 1551 is given together with texts from the Reformers that were found objectionable.

When one looks at the texts from which the Tridentine articles were excerpted, one notices that the objections of the Reformers centred around the notion of *ex opere operato* efficacy. This was not taken as an abstract notion, corrosive of doctrinal purity, but as a practical issue, affecting not only church teaching but also practices. As the statement *Das Herrenmahl* of 1978 notes, the two particular matters which

---

[3] On the use of the Reformers' writings at Trent, and on the extent to which they were known, cf. Theobald Freudenberger, 'Zur Benützung des reformatorischen Schriftums im Konzil von Trient', in Remigius Bäumer, *Von Konstanz nach Trient: Beiträge zur Geschichte der Kirche von den Reformkonzilien bis zum Tridentinum* (München-Paderborn-Wien: Ferdinand Schöningh 1972) 577–601.

[4] CT VI/I 323 8–325 11.

caught the Reformers' attention were private mass and the infrequency of communion among the faithful, two points which they saw to be intimately connected, and linked with the teaching on *ex opere operato* efficacy.[5] We are used to hearing or reading quotations from Martin Luther in which he inveighed against abuses and the greed of the clergy, but it is important to remember that for him the fundamental abuse was the private mass itself, not just its lucrative aspects. On the Catholic side, the concern with practice was just as great and as emotional. In the course of the decades given to the holding of the Council, many abuses of the mass were corrected, but the fundamental institution that allowed private mass and mass offerings was always upheld and supported, even when communion was encouraged.

From the outset, any examination of the teaching of Trent on the mass, or any consideration of its dogmas, has to keep in mind that doctrine and practice belong essentially together. The Conciliar participants were not talking about the eucharist in an abstract way, but they discussed it and explained it as they saw it practised, and in view of the reformation practices which they saw challenging the established ones. Similarly the objections of the Reformers to catholic doctrine were allied with objections to specific practices. In arguing over doctrine, both sides were simultaneously arguing for a practice or for its abolition.

Early articles were derived from the writings of Martin Luther, Ioannes Aepinus and the *Confessio Augustana*. For the moment, it is enough to look at the points from these writings as they were quoted. Later, it will be necessary to make further comment on the Reformation position.

In its repudiation of private masses, that is of any mass celebrated without communion of the faithful, the *Confessio Augustana* refers back to the need for justification by faith. If, it

---

[5] *Das Herrenmahl*, Exkurse 3 and 4, 93–105: *The Eucharist*, 69–80.

says, the mass can *ex opere operato take away the sins of the living and the dead*, it follows that justification is by the work of the mass and not by faith.[6] It decries the multiplication of private masses, which it claims is supported by the theory that by his passion Christ satisfied for original sin but instituted the mass to be offered for daily sins.[7] Aepinus, for his part, is quoted as saying that it was never the intention of the church to beseech pardon and to satisfy for sins by means of the mass, whether by way of supplication or by way of applying satisfaction.[8] In this, as will be seen, he refers to a disputed point among medieval divines on the way in which the mass abrogates sin. Luther, of course, is on record for his treatise on the abrogation of the private mass and for his objections to the idea of applying the fruits of the mass for people other than the communicants.[9]

The articles excerpted from the 'heretics' in 1551 included even more references to Reformation writings, adding to those already mentioned the names of Bucer, Calvin, Zwingli and Melanchton. To take only the example of what is quoted from the *Confessio Augustana* in the *Acta*, we find it saying that, despite all the testimonies from the past quoted by catholic apologists, there is no proof that the mass gives grace *ex opere operato* or that, applied for others, it can merit remission of sins,

---

[6] *Confessio Augustana* 24, 29: 'Si missa tollit peccata vivorum ac mortuorum ex opere operato, contingit iustificatio ex opere missarum, non ex fide.' This and the following texts are found in CT, l. c.

[7] ibid., 24, 21: 'Accessit opinio, quae auxit privatas missas in infinitum, videlicet quod Christus sua passione satisfecerit pro peccato originali et instituit missam, in qua fieret oblatio pro quotidianis delictis mortalibus et venialibus.'

[8] Ioannes Aepinus, *Propositiones contra fanaticas et sacrilegas opiniones Papisticorum dogmatum de missa*, no. 65: 'Missis privatis aut in modum supplicationis aut satisfactionis applicatis non solum vivis ac mortuis velle impetrare veniam, sed et velle Deo satisfacere, ecclesiae Dei intentio nunquam fuit nec est nec erit.'

[9] Martin Luther, *De abroganda missa privata*, LW 36, 311ff.

whether it be the fault or the punishment due to them.[10] The idea of an application of the mass's merit to those who place no obstacle to grace (*non ponentibus obicem*) is scorned.[11]

It is currently discussed whether the Reformers were arguing against quaint and superstitious practices, and against the poor theology that seemed to support them, or whether there was a fundamental difference between catholics and reformers on the sacrificial nature of the mass, that still worries full sacramental reconciliation between churches. It is not a simple question to answer, because in the course of polemics issues are muddled, and likewise because the historical knowledge that we have of sacramental and religious practice in the centuries immediately preceding the schisms of the sixteenth century is still not complete or clear. In order, therefore, to get a more accurate view of what was debated at Trent, and so of what was there taught against the reformers, it will be useful to look at late medieval mass practices and to give an outline of the theology of the *ex opere operato* efficacy of the mass in later medieval writers, together with a glimpse at the work of the sixteenth century catholic apologists.

*Background to Trent: Late Medieval Mass Practices*
One cannot discuss late medieval mass practices without taking the entire religious construct of which they were a part into consideration. Two quotations can serve to give a bird's eye view of what this was. First, there is Steven Ozment's reckoning of that to which the Protestant Reformation brought an end:

---

[10] *Apologia Confessionis Augustanae*, art. 24: '. . . non ostendat quod missa ex opere operato conferat gratiam, aut applicata pro aliis mereatur eis remissionem venialium et mortalium peccatorum, culpae et poenae.'

[11] ibid.: 'Repudiandi sunt et reliqui communes errores, quod missa conferat gratiam ex opere operato facienti. Item quod applicatio pro aliis etiam iniustis, non ponentibus obicem, mereatur eis remissionem peccatorum, culpae et poenae.'

... Protestants proposed a revolution in religious concept, practice, and institutions. Even in its modest forms the Reformation called for, and in most Protestant areas permanently achieved, an end to mandatory fasting; auricular confession; the worship of saints, relics, and images; indulgences; pilgrimages and shrines; vigils; weekly, monthly, and annual masses for the dead; the belief in purgatory; Latin worship services; the sacrifice of the Mass; numerous religious ceremonies, festivals, and holidays; the canonical hours; monasteries and mendicant orders; the sacraments of marriage, extreme unction, confirmation, holy orders, and penance; clerical celibacy; clerical immunity from civil taxation and criminal jurisdiction; nonresident benefices; excommunication and interdict; canon law; episcopal and papal authority; and the traditional scholastic education of the clergy.[12]

On the other hand, there is Francis Oakley's bemused summing-up of a whole host of religious observances, only now being brought to clearer light as a result of detailed local investigations:

As the evidence continues to accumulate—evidence concerning the quality of popular preaching, the survival in the villages of magical and quasi-pagan practices, the activities of confraternities, the nature of legacies left for religious purposes, the means of religious instruction (liturgical, theatrical catechetical, penitential), the range of liturgical and paraliturgical rites, and the dissemination of popular devotional literature—it is hard to know what to make of it, what to compare it with, from what perspective to view it.[13]

View it, of course, scholars do, and often indeed in different

[12] Steven E. Ozment, *The Reformation in the Cities: The Appeal of Protestantism to Sixteenth-Century Germany and Switzerland* (New Haven & London: Yale University Press 1975) 117f.
[13] Francis Oakley, 'Religious and Ecclesiastical Life on the Eve of the Reformation', in Steven E. Ozment (ed.), *Reformation Europe: A Guide to Research* (St. Louis: Center for Reformation Research 1982) 20.

ways. Few seem to disagree that there were exaggerations, gross impieties, clerical negligence, not a little touch of the magical, and consequently things that needed reform. There is disagreement, however, in judging the basic health of the religious system. Despite the abuses, did it provide a setting in which people's fundamental religious and cultural needs could be served, in general fidelity to the institutions of Christ, or did it constitute a system so corrupt that it needed some sort of radical reform? Furthermore, when Protestant and Catholic reformers set about their respective tasks were they both, despite their acerbic differences, trying to salvage the same fundamental faith, the same order of grace, and the traditional evangelical religious practices, such as true prayer, baptism and the right celebration of the Lord's Supper? Or did they disagree substantially on matters of justification, on the order of worship, on the nature of the eucharist, and on the divine ordinances concerning ministry?

Here, we only have to deal with the eucharist, and even more specifically with its sacrificial character. The question then is whether at the heart of the mass system, by all accounts in need of reform, catholics still found an understanding of sacrifice which they saw as fundamental to eucharistic theology and practice and therefore to be preserved, an understanding however which the Reformers could by no means accept. The alternative view is that both parties actually agreed on fundamentals about the eucharist, but quarrelled because they approached the reform from different perspectives and with different tactics.

There seem at present to be three historical viewpoints on the religious practices of the pre-Reformation period and on their relation to the Reformation itself. First of all, there are those who in looking at the late medieval religious system, including its mass and eucharistic practices, place them in their cultural setting and find that the system generally met the religious and social needs of people and communities.[14] In this respect, their approach is more positive than was that of earlier historians, who saw this period as one of decay.[15] Secondly, there are those catholic historians who think that the fourteenth and fifteenth centuries betrayed what had been ecclesiastically and theologically established in the twelfth and thirteenth, and that it was abuse and decadence that led to the need for reform, and also provided the Reformers with a target for their criticism.[16] They sometimes surmise that the protestants were fighting against abuses, whereas catholic apologists were trying to retrieve the early medieval understanding and system of church life and spirituality. Thirdly, there are those historians who believe that the corruption of religious practice and faith that led to the attempts at reform was the inevitable outcome of what had come to the fore in the twelfth and thirteenth centuries, so that differences between the catholic party and reformers were indeed deep and fundamental. On the mass, in particular, Oakley lists those critical changes of the late-antique and early medieval periods which lie at the base of the mass-system and which were unacceptable to the Reform: 'changes that had conspired to make the consecration of the mass the focus, the action of the priest's rather than the people's, the sacrifice a repetition, the benefit a quantity, the number a consideration'.[17] From this point of view, what broke away from the system was an achievement, a new won freedom, a claim to a place in the church for the people, a new attentiveness to the Gospel. The

---

[14] For example, John Bossy, 'Essai de sociographie de la messe, 1200–1700', *Annales. Economies, Sociétés. Civilisations* 36 (1981) 44–70; Natalie Z. Davis, 'The Sacred and the Body Social in 16th century Lyon', *Past and Present* 90 (1981) 40–70.

[15] Cf. Ozment, *The Reformation* . . . on trends in reformation studies, 1–14.

[16] This trend is linked with the name of Joseph Lortz, who began to re-examine the positions of the reformers in the light of catholic corruption and abuse.

[17] Oakley, l.c. 21, note 81.

Reformers of the sixteenth century, while certainly bringing insights and strategies of their own, simply built on attempts at change that had been made in the preceding centuries. As precedent to the Reformation, one could list movements that fostered lay spirituality and initiative, and theologies such as those of Scotus and Ockham, that supported the freedom of the individual and freed the means of grace from the priestly system that took hold both ecclesiastically and theologically from the eleventh to thirteenth centuries. Of these theologies, Steven Ozment writes:

> In the teaching of Scotus and Ockham, traditional religious institutions ceased to be the essential link in a great hierarchical chain of being. Their uniqueness lay rather in a contingent divine act; from an infinite number of theoretical possibilities God had chosen them to be the instruments of his will in time. For those who subscribed to such a point of view the things of religion were only as real as one could believe them to be. From Luther to the American Puritans the central religious problem of mainstream Protestantism became the certitude of salvation— not the rationality of faith or the proof of God's existence, but the trustworthiness of God's word and promise.[18]

In looking, then, to the teaching of Trent on the sacrifice of the mass, as one would also have to do on other scores, it is necessary to ask whether in the theology and mass system that preceded the Reformation attack apologists found, despite the abuses which they too wished to correct, a core of belief and practice which they defended against the Reformation, and which the reformers did in truth wish to abolish. In order to answer this question, it is helpful to look in a little more detail at some of the practices that local historians have uncovered in the

---

[18] Steven E. Ozment, *The Age of Reform 1250–1550: An Intellectual and Religious History of Late Medieval and Reformation Europe* (New Haven and London: Yale University Press 1980) 244.

times preceding, during and immediately after the holding of the Council.

Indeed, one already gets some idea of what practices were in vogue from the lists of what were considered abuses drawn up from Reformers working in particular churches. Early in the reform, in December 1521, the city council of Wittenberg proposed to the elector, Frederick, that there should be an end to prescribed or endowed masses, 'since many priests must say five, six, seven, or even more masses daily'.[19] They likewise asked for the 'abolition of all requiem, burial, anniversary, confraternal, marriage, and votive Masses', giving as their reason that 'the Mass benefits only those who are physically present to receive it'.[20] Drawing up a list of needed reforms in religious practice for the Margrave George of Brandenburg-Ansbach, Johann Rurer of Ansbach included this list of abuses in the use of the mass as a propitiatory sacrifice: the daily offering of the sacrifice for the sins of the living and the dead, the payment for the celebration of masses, foundation masses that were obligatory on priests, reception of communion by the priest alone, and saying of mass in a language unknown to the people.

The things included in such lists would have been recognized by all as common practice. It is the judgement that they constituted abuses that was the point of quarrel, for catholic apologists argued that substantially they corresponded to the nature of the mass, whatever the correctives that needed to be applied to remove exaggerations. The reformation teaching that the mass or Lord's Supper was a testament and a promise of God's forgiveness showed up these practices and the doctrine that founded them as blasphemous, but the catholic teaching that the mass as offered by a priest was a propitiatory sacrifice supported them. Indeed, it was this persuasion, whether

[19] Cf. Ozment, *The Reformation* . . . 143.
[20] ibid.

proposed in theological teaching or embraced in popular credence, that lay at the heart of a rather complex mass system, which is best known to us from local histories.[21]

One of the more central practices of this system was to guarantee the celebration of the mass for the dead as well as for the living, to offer satisfaction for their sins and to plead for their eternal rest. Not only did the living have to make such provisions for the dead, but people often provided the foundation of masses for themselves in their wills and bequests. In a study of religious practice in sixteenth-century Champagne, A. Galpern gives the example of the provisions made in the will of a rich woman, Damoiselle Guillemette Coquillant, wife of an attorney of Reims. For the day of her death, she ordered along with the prayers for the commendation of her soul, the celebration of thirty low masses. For the day of her burial, she wanted three masses, and for the day of her principal service, which would be the Sunday following her death, she ordered three solemn masses and thirty low masses. For a year after that, a daily low mass would be said in her parish church for the remedy of her own soul and those of her late relatives and friends, culminating in one high and thirty low requiem masses on the day of her anniversary.[22] Not all persons would have been able to afford such generous bounty to their own souls, but apparently this will gives a good example of

---

[21] Cf. Oakley, art. cit., 21: 'Nor for the proper understanding of popular piety in the later Middle Ages, does the future necessarily lie with either medievalists or Reformation historians as such. Rather, it seems likely to lie with those who, in pursuing the detailed local investigations we still need, are self-conscious about the dangers of anachronism, hesitant about distinguishing too confidently between "religion" and "superstition", and open in their interpretations to the insights of the sociologists, cultural anthropologists, and students of comparative religion.'

[22] A. N. Galpern, *The Religion of the People in Sixteenth-Century Champagne* (Cambridge: Cambridge University Press 1976) 21ff.

how the living did provide for their own spiritual needs after death.

Other points in Damoiselle Coquillant's will illustrate further components of what was a coherent religious system. In foreseeing her funeral service, she made provisions for the participation of the poor of the town. They were to be given material help in return for their prayers and their presence at her services. Apparently, this was done not only out of the lady's charity for the poor, but also out of the persuasion that their prayers would be helpful, or, in other words, out of a sense of christian solidarity in the spiritual as well as the material. Similarly, she made provisions to have offices performed for her in convents and by confraternities, of which there were a considerable number in the parish.

A striking point in this will, as in others, is that the testator could obviously rely on a large number of clergy, either secular or regular, who would be available to take part in services and to celebrate masses. This does seem to give a reasonably accurate picture of the profusion of clergy at that time, something that on the one hand seemed necessary to the religious system but that on the other laid the way open to turning the mass and other religious services into a business, since these were the primary source of priestly revenue. Rather, however, than giving us a picture of the people dominated by the clergy, it gives an impression of clergy at the beck and call of the people.

Another aspect of the mass system, as part of a greater whole, is its connection with the cult of the saints. This is illustrated for us in a book about religious practice in sixteenth-century Spain by W. Christian.[23] From the abuses condemned by the reformers and from the canons of the Council of Trent, we know of the custom of celebrating mass in honour of the saints,

---

[23] William A. Christian, *Local Religion in Sixteenth-Century Spain* (Princeton: Princeton University Press 1981).

or more particularly of the Virgin Mary. Sometimes, this took the form of vowed masses. That is to say, at a time of need or calamity a village, town or city appealed to the intercession of the local patron and made a public pledge or vow to have masses celebrated in her or his honour, in the course of a public observance of their feast.[24] Thus the satisfaction offered to God in the mass for sin would be joined with the prayers and intercession of God's special friends, the saints. It was hoped in this way to avert natural and human-made calamities.

Though the sixteenth century reformers saw all this as an abuse of and a departure from true evangelical faith and religion, one cannot hope to understand the meaning of the mass, and of its offering as sacrifice, unless one takes the motivational factors into account. In other words, one can ask what was the common belief, or set of beliefs, that held persuasive strength for the religious life of peoples, and that thus made sense out of the uses to which they put the offering of mass.[25]

At the root of the religious belief and practice there seems to have been a particular persuasion about God's relation to the universe and to human life. God was believed to have direct control of cosmic and natural forces and of the lives of societies and individual persons. All that happened, whether good or bad, was attributed to the exercise of divine power. Since the centuries immediately preceding the Reformation were a time of war, famine, plague and other natural calamities, people were prone to see God's anger in all of this and consequently to heighten their own sense of sinfulness. Hence the devotion to Christ, which was a strongly affectionate one, took on a deep penitential colouring, and appeal to the patronage of the saints

[24] See the example of the Madrid vow, July 25, 1597, in Christian, op. cit. 209.
[25] See above, note 14.

in averting disaster and providing protection was common. For a society that lived on the practices of patronage, it was not unnatural to cast the saints in similar mould. Since life was precarious and death always imminent, these centuries also show a great fascination with death and with the art of dying, and this carried over into a great feeling of solidarity between the living and the dead. People were convinced that the dead could render service to the living, and vice versa, so that the offering of masses in suffrage for the departed was a particularly solid way of demonstrating solidarity. In other words, the sense of social coherence took in not only the living, divided according to rank and class, each having a due role to play, but also the dead, both the patron saints and people's own relatives and friends.

Consequently, when one looks back to the accusations of abuse levied by the reformers, and particularly to the accusation that this was an unevangelical religion, or that it relied on human works, one has to attend to the judgment of local historians that the system did give coherence and meaning, and even hope, to life, and that this system was one that allowed people to live in a world that they saw wholly in God's hands. On the other hand, one may also appreciate the burdens of belief and grasp the fact that the reformers rebelled not only against poor doctrine and blasphemous practice, but against a whole cultural and social system that appeared oppressive to personal freedom and to deprive the individual of a more direct and personal access to the mercy of God. Catholic apologists tried to keep the old system going, with a correction of excesses and superstitions. The reformers had to take on the task, not only of purifying belief and practice in some vital areas, but of putting a whole new devotional and cultural system in place.

Of course, in a time of actual change and development, made more complex by altercation and polemics, nothing is neatly sorted out in the minds of the agents of change, and attention does have to focus quite often on particulars. As far as mass practice was concerned, there is no doubt that the positions of the reformers were influenced by the rather poor theology of the fruits of the mass that some writers offered in justification of mass offering. Hence, we should look at that theology.

### Background to Trent: Late Medieval Theology of the Mass[26]

In terms such as merit, *ex opere operato*, satisfaction and application, quoted in the writings of the reformation, we do indeed recognize the vocabulary of catholic theology on the mass in the preceding centuries. This theology is tied up with the influence of the penitential system, and with its emphasis on making satisfaction for sins already absolved. An outline of the major points of the theology of the fruits of the mass is given in what follows.

First of all, when the term *ex opere operato* is used to explain the bestowal of grace through the sacraments, and this is promised to those who simply place no obstacle (*obex*), inadequate attention seems to have been given to the acts and dispositions of the subject, though the origins of the term in earlier scholastic theology had to do with the triumph of the grace of Christ, which worked through the sacraments, over the unworthiness of the sinner. When the term was used to indicate the efficacy of the application of the mass to someone for the remission of sin, the idea was that the efficacy of the mass's application paralleled the efficacy of sacramental reception.

Secondly, since the merits and satisfactions of Christ on the cross were considered to be of infinite value, it had to be explained why the mass could be offered for particular persons and why such application could be repeated for the same person.

---

[26] Cf. Erwin Iserloh, 'Der Wert der Messe in der Diskussion der Theologen vom Mittelalter bis zum 16. Jahrhundert', *Zeitschrift für katholische Theologie* 83 (1961) 44–79.

In other words, the finite value of application had to be reconciled with the infinite value of the merits or satisfactions of Christ, which were applied. A number of writers had recourse to a distinction between the value of the sacrifice of the cross *ex sese* and the value of its representation in the mass. When Christ, it was held, offered himself on the cross this sacrifice was offered for the sins of the whole world and was of infinite value. When its representation, however, is offered by the priest, according to these writers, he acts in the name of the church and the offering is of limited value. The representation cannot be equated with the original offering.

Furthermore, to deal with the issue of limited value in the continued application of the mass, either for the same person or for different persons, theologians distinguished between the mass's application *per modum suffragii* and its application *per modum satisfactionis*. The satisfaction made by Christ to God can be meted out to sinners, but the response to intercession or suffrage depends totally on the response of the divine mercy. Behind this distinction regarding the offering of the mass there lay the thought that there was a double aspect to Christ's redemptive act on the cross. On the one hand, he was deemed to have made satisfaction in justice for the offence rendered to God by sin. On the other, he was pictured as making priestly intercession, imploring the intervention of the divine mercy beyond the limits of justice. Hence in the mass, the application of satisfaction for sin belonged to the order of justice and is in some way measurable, but it is possible that God in mercy may respond to the intercession of Christ and the church beyond the limits of what is due in justice.

The image of satisfaction is thus quantitative, and nestles in the context of penitential computations.[27] When in the ordering

---

[27] For a good explanation of how the development of the private mass relates to the penitential system, cf. Cyrille Vogel, 'Une mutation cultuelle

of penance according to the celtic system of tariff penance, penances of fast and prayer over a period of time were meted out, it was possible to commute these penances by offering a fixed number of masses or praying a designated number of psalms. The penitential books indicated what these equivalents were, e.g. twenty masses can compensate for seven months of penance. The theology of satisfaction as applied to the redemption by Christ and as applied to the application of the mass invokes this kind of quantitative imagery. A particular use of this is found in the distinction between the remission of the sin itself and the remission of the punishment due to it, or between the *culpa* and the *poena*. Thus, some writers held that the mass is propitiatory in as much as it reconciles sinners to God, but satisfactory in as much as it pays the debt due to sin, or in other words serves to commute the penance that a sinner would normally have to undertake. For other writers, the question is more complicated: they ask whether the application of the mass can be made for punishment alone, or for punishment of all sin and the remission of venial sin, or for the remission even of venial sin. In answer to this question, they make various uses of the distinction between suffrage and satisfaction, since what cannot be obtained by way of making satisfaction may well be obtainable through intercession.

In explanations given of the limits of the fruits applied through any one mass, the measure of what was given turned out to be the devotion of the church. The church was taken to be the offerer of the cross's representation in the mass, the church here being understood as the social body of those living on earth at any given time. The devotion of such a body is both limited and varied, and this helped to explain why the value of the mass's offering was both limited and varied, whatever the

inexpliquée: le passage de l'eucharistie communautaire à la messe privée', *Revue des Sciences Religieuses* 54 (1980) 231–250.

infinite value of the sacrifice represented. Some writers even suggested that the actual priest-celebrant had an effect on the application and its fruits, since his own merit or devotion entered into account. In this case also, the distinction between suffrage and satisfaction was applied: the priest's devotion might not affect the quantity of satisfaction applied but did indeed affect what was obtained by way of intercession.

This was the kind of theology known apparently to the Reformers, who often cite Gabriel Biel. No doubt an explanation of the sacrifice that did not appeal to such measurings and seem to rely so much on the devotion, or even merit of the church, could have allayed some of their fears. Iserloh points out that though there were catholic theologians in the sixteenth century who did not resort to this theology, the Reformers continued to appeal to it in making their objections against the mass.[28] In any case, was this mathematically minded theology the real source of their problems with the mass, or did they have deeper objections to the idea itself that the mass is a sacrifice of propitiation? Some consideration of the catholic apologists who took up the controversy with the protestants may help to answer this question.[29]

In the works of such men as Kaspar Schatzgeyer, Michael Helding, or Silvester Prierias, there is little of the kind of calculatory approach outlined above. For them, the mass was a mystical, sacramental and representative offering, wholly related to the sacrifice of the cross, of which it is the memorial. Their theology was built totally on belief in the real presence of

[28] art. cit. Cf. also V. Pfnür, l.c.

[29] Cf. Erwin Iserloh, 'Das Tridentinische Messopferdekret in seinem Beziehungen zu der Kontroverstheologie der Zeit', in *Il Concilio di Trento e la Riforma Cattolica. Atti del Convegno Storico Internazionale, Trento 2–6 settembre 1963* (Rome 1965) vol. 2, 401–439; M. Lepin, *L'Idée du Sacrifice de la Messe d'après les théologiens depuis l'origine jusqu'à nos jours* (Paris: Beauchesne 1926) 252–292.

Christ in the eucharist, under the species of bread and wine, so that if the doctrine of the real presence were attacked so also was the doctrine of the eucharistic sacrifice. There were different ways in which the apologists related the offering of Christ in the mass to the sacrifice of the cross. One group related it more directly to the Last Supper, or to the offering which Christ made of himself at the supper, before suffering on the cross. For them, it was this offering that was sacramentally represented in the mass, but because of the real presence it could be said that it was the victim of the sacrifice of the cross that was offered. For another group, it was the offering on the cross itself that was mystically represented on the altar through the action of the priest, so that consecration and offering coincided. For still a third group, it was the heavenly offering of Christ, the eternal high-priest, that was sacramentally represented, that continuous offering which he makes of himself to the Father, in virtue of the once-for-all spilling of his blood on the cross. For the majority of the apologists, therefore, there is no sense in which an oblation or work of the church could be separated from the once-for-all sacrifice of Christ on the cross.

The sacramental representation and commemoration of the cross did, however, in their view, make the offering of mass by the priest for the living and the dead possible, and they did not see this as running counter to the need of faith and devotion in those who received the graces of Christ's death. They felt, indeed, that the account given by the reformers of the catholic doctrine of the *ex opere operato* efficacy of the mass-offering was a farce. However, already in the *Confutatio* of the Augsburg Confession we find catholic apologists standing up for private mass and for the language that allowed the mass to be a sacrifice of propitiation,[30] and this continued through the controversy of

---

[30] Cf. Jared Wicks, 'Abuses under Indictment at the Diet of Augsburg 1530', *Theological Studies* 41 (1980) 300.

the years preceding the convocation of the Council of Trent.
Whatever about his earlier conciliatory attitudes, in the
response to the *Confutatio* in his *Apologia* for the Augsburg
confession Melanchton gives a long and often bitter refutation
of the teaching that the mass is a sacrifice of propitiation,[31] since
he seemed to think that the very designation of the mass in this
way necessarily involved a theology of merit through works.
The protestant distinction between the sacrifice of thanksgiving
and praise on the one hand and the sacrifice of propitiation on
the other was thus an important and fundamental one, for the
former term could be used of the eucharist, and was often used
of it, but the latter belonged to the cross alone.

Beyond this point, there is some disagreement between
contemporary interpreters of the *Confessio Augustana* and of
Melanchton's *Apologia*. Vilmos Vajta can say that the *sacrificium
propitiatorium* of Christ is *hic et nunc* present in the sacramental
form of bread and wine, according to reformation doctrine,
when this is expressed in contemporary words.[32] Erwin Iserloh,
however, thinks that Melanchton displayed a rather more
fundamental opposition to any usage of propitiatory language.
He points out that in the *Apologia* the eucharist itself is never
called a sacrifice, for it is in itself sacrament, and that where the
language of sacrifice is taken to be tolerable Melanchton refers
to such things as the preaching of the gospel, faith, prayer,

---

[31] Cf. *The Book of Concord: Confessions of the Evangelical Lutheran Church*,
translated and edited by Theodore G. Tappert (Philadelphia: Fortress 1976)
249–268.

[32] Vilmos Vajta, 'Das Abëndmahl. Gegenwart Christi—Feier der
Gemeinschaft—eucharistisches Opfer', in *Confessio Augustana und Confutatio:
der Augsburger Reichstag 1530 und die Einheit der Kirche*, in Verbindung mit
Barbara Hellensleben herausgegeben van Erwin Iserloh (Münster: Aschendorf
1980) 573: 'Als *sacrificium propitiatorium* wird einzig Christi Kreuzestod
bezeichnet. Dass jedoch dieses Opfer unter der Gestalt des Brotes und Weines
als *hic et nunc* gegenwärtig wird, ist in der CA und in der Apologie
nachdrücklich bejaht'.

thanksgiving, the afflictions of the saints, and all their good works.[33] These, however, are things that accompany the celebration of the eucharistic sacrament, and in no way constitute the sacrament itself. Iserloh finds such a strong opposition in Melanchton to application *ex opere operato* that he could not allow in any way for a sacrificial designation of the sacrament itself. This opposition to the application of the mass by a priest, or to having the mass applied for those not present, may indicate the most fundamental problem in the whole debate about the mass.

It is somewhat surprising to read the following very irenic account of things in a joint article by Vajta and Iserloh:

> What was disputed was whether in the Mass we, as a congregation with Christ as the head, offer to the Father the onetime propitiatory sacrifice for the sin of the world. According to the Reformation view, the sacrifice of praise and thanksgiving, which the congregation in the celebration of the Lord's Supper offered through Christ in the Holy Spirit, was its only access to the Father opened up through Christ's sacrifice on the Cross. The question Catholic theologians posed in return continued to be whether the movement by which the congregation through, with, and in Christ comes before the Father is here fully seen. Does not the church in the Mass offer the onetime propitiatory sacrifice in sacramental form? . . .[34]

This, in truth, seems to be only half the picture, for it leaves out the heavy protestant emphasis on sacramental proclamation and reception, and the catholic contention about offering for others, as well as its defence of the private mass as essential to a

[33] In *Confessio Augustana* . . . 581f., in the discussion on the paper by Vajta.
[34] Erwin Iserloh and Vilmos Vajta, 'The Sacraments: Baptism and the Lord's Supper', in *Confessing One Faith: A Joint Commentary on the Augsburg Confession by Lutheran and Catholic Theologians*, edited by George W. Forell and James F. McCue (Minneapolis: Augsburg 1982) 216.

traditional devotion and practice. In any case to understand how Trent approached debates about the mass it seems possible to list the main problems that the reformers had with catholic teaching and practice:

(a) they raised problems about an apparently automatic application of Christ's satisfaction, i.e., without faith or devotion in the one to whom the application was made;

(b) they objected to the idea that the eucharist could benefit non-communicants, not only among those present at the mass but also among the absent, not only the living but also the dead;

(c) they objected to the importance given to the act of the celebrating priest, where it looked as if this act was effectively divorced from the community's participation and the mass took on the form of a private celebration;

(d) they questioned the propitiatory character of the mass as such, seeing in this idea an instance of works' theology, so that even when the objections over the dispositions required in the recipients of satisfaction were answered a more fundamental problem remained;

(e) they took exception to the invocation of the saints and to the celebration of masses in their honour, finding in these practices a substitution of the works of the saints for the satisfaction of Christ.

Melanchton seems to have summed up the controversy when he wrote in the *Apology*:

> We are perfectly willing for the Mass to be understood as a daily sacrifice, provided this means the whole Mass, the ceremony and also the proclamation of the Gospel, faith, prayer and thanksgiving. Taken together, these are the daily sacrifice of the New Testament; the ceremony was instituted because of them and ought not to be separated from them. Therefore Paul says (1 Cor 11.26), 'As often as you eat this bread and drink this cup, you proclaim the Lord's death.' From the Levitical analogy it does not follow at all that there must be a ceremony that justifies

*ex opere operato* or that merits the forgiveness of sins when applied to others.[35]

On the one hand, this is a very irenical statement. On the other, it shows where exactly the division stood between catholics and reformers. At the heart of Lutheran worship was the proclamation of the Gospel and the sacrament of the body and blood, given for the forgiveness of sins. The one thing that was excluded from the idea of sacrifice was that this body and blood could be offered to God and that it could obtain, by the offering, the remission of sins for non-communicants. The catholic position was that the priestly act of proclaiming the words of Christ at the Last Supper was itself a sacrifice, or at least an essential part of it, for some writers spoke of the consecration alone as the sacrifice and others of the consecration together with the words of offering that followed it. As we will see, while the Council of Trent did not stand by the use of *ex opere operato* terminology for the offering of the sacrifice, it stood by the interpretation of the priest's act as a sacrifice, beneficial to those for whom it was offered by the intention of the minister.

*Conclusion*
In this chapter, we have looked at the practice of mass in the centuries preceding the reformation, as well as at two different types of theology with which the reformers ought to have been familiar. We have also considered the objections from the reformers taken up by the Council of Trent. All of these considerations constitute an important background to the Council's own discussions and definitions.

[35] Apology of the Augsburg Confession, *The Book of Concord* 256.

Chapter 3

## THE COUNCIL IN SESSION 1547–1552

Against the background of practice, theology and reformers' questions outlined in the previous chapter, we have to ask how the theologians and bishops understood the issues, when the Council of Trent took up the debate on the sacrifice of the mass. Erwin Iserloh has noted an important difference between the way in which the question was approached during the session at Bologna in 1547 and then at Trent in 1551/52. At Bologna, according to him, the main concern of the speakers was to show that the mass as a representation of the sacrifice of the cross could itself be termed a sacrifice of propitiation. In 1551/52 on the contrary, speakers tended to demonstrate how the mass had its efficacy precisely as an application of the offering of the cross.[1] In other words, in the second debate the sacramental relation between mass and cross was more directly discussed and perceived than in the first. For brevity's sake, however, we will here consider the arguments and proposals of the two sessions together, while being careful to note these two possible ways of debating the issue.

### The Articles Debated

Mention was already made in the last chapter of the articles which had been excerpted from the writings of the reformers and put to the theologians for discussion and censure. We have also considered some of the practices and theologies of the centuries immediately preceding the reformation, since this casts light on how the protestant objections are to be understood. To put the question about propitiatory sacrifice

[1] Iserloh, 'Das Tridentinische Messopferdekret . . .', l.c. 416f.

and about its efficacy in proper context all the articles proposed for debate have to be taken into account. In other words, to do justice to the issue, one cannot effectively distinguish between the articles on doctrine and those on practical matters. The sense of the doctrinal issues can be understood only in conjunction with the argument over right practice.

The first of the articles presented at Bologna is addressed in broad terms to the sacrificial nature of the mass. The reformers are quoted as saying that the mass is a mere commemoration of the sacrifice of the cross, and that it is in no way an offering for sin. The second article already demonstrates the practical side of controversy, for it questions the traditional piety which allowed for the application of masses for the living and the dead. The third article presents the practice of taking mass offerings or stipends in the worst possible light, saying that the mass as practised by catholics or papists has been invented for the sake of gain. It has no foundation in the gospel and it is not possible to attribute the mass to Christ's institution.

In composing the fourth article, the Council's aides had in mind the broadsides of the reformers against the multiplication of private masses. It is closely linked to the fifth, which cites attacks against those masses at which only the priest-celebrant communicates. In fact, this was the general sense given to the term *private mass*, at the time, though some of the speakers at the Council also defended what one might more properly call the celebration of masses in private, without the presence of any faithful. The reformers opposed the celebration of mass wherein only a priest received communion, whether said before the people or in a private place.

The sixth article synopsizes the attacks against the Roman *Canon Missae*, calling it a collection of pernicious errors, dangerous to the memory of the cross. From their writings, it is clear that such reformers as Martin Luther and Ulrich Zwingli found support for mass-offerings in the canon. That was how they understood all the verbs of offering that occur both before and after the institution narrative, then commonly thought of as the words of consecration or as the sacramental form of the eucharist. In saying such a prayer, the priest seemed to presume either to offer Christ all over again, or to add another offering to the offering of the cross.[2] Finally, the seventh article presented for discussion records the attacks against the unevangelical nature of mixing water with wine in the celebration of the eucharist.

In this listing of alleged errors, the place given to practices is very important. The second, third, fourth and fifth articles indicate very clearly what practical concerns the conciliar theologians saw to be behind the doctrinal controversies. What it was proposed to defend at the Council was traditional catholic practice and its foundation in the teaching that had been developed about the propitiatory nature of the eucharistic sacrifice. Few of those who attended mass received communion, yet they were believed to obtain benefit from it. Many masses were offered by priests without attendant congregations, in return for an alms or a stipend, and these were considered to avail to the salvation of those for whom they were offered. Such practices seemed to stand or fall on the defence of the mass as a priestly offering of propitiation, an act advantageous to the church as a whole and to the single faithful, who could safely turn to it to obtain pardon and grace, both for themselves and for others, living and deceased.[3]

The attack on the Canon of the mass and its defence also pin-

[2] See the Analysis of the Canon in Martin Luther, 'The Abomination of the Secret Mass', *Luther's Works*, vol. 36, 311ff.

[3] In the earlier sessions of the Council, one finds no great anxiety on the part of the speakers to increase the frequency of communion among the laity. It is only in the later sessions that voice is given to this concern. This itself is indicative of what the bishops and theologians had in mind in defending the propitiatory character of the mass.

point the nature of the controversy. As mentioned, this had to do with the reading of the canon as an act of offering, performed for the church by its agent, the priest. It was attacked because it was understood to be so, and it was defended for the same reason. Finally, the article about mixing water with wine in its own way reflects one of the central points of the Reformation debate, namely, the appeal to the scriptures as the necessary adjudication of all beliefs and practices.

When the Council took up the question of the sacrifice of the mass after its reconvention at Trent in 1551, the theologians were again asked to give their answer to a list of articles drawn from Reformation writings. This time, they were asked to deal with these along with a series of errors concerning the sacrament of order. Their instructions were to present arguments to refute the heretical positions, drawing them from scripture, apostolic traditions, councils, popes, fathers of the church, and finally from whatever source could be said to represent the universal consent of the Catholic Church.[4]

This time, the articles on the mass were ten in number,[5] but they were not substantially different from what had been gathered together in 1547, though more reformers were named in this list. The first three articles represent the doctrinal side of the controversy, with the same accent on the propitiatory character of the mass. The other articles have to do with the practices that went along with this belief. Articles four to eight inclusive repeat the concerns that had faced the speakers at Bologna. In the meantime, other accusations against the mass had been recorded, and these are mentioned in articles nine and ten. The first of these mentions accusations against the silent

---

[4] CT VII/I 114 9–11: 'Sententiae per theologos dicendae deducantur ex sacra scriptura, traditionibus apostolicis, sacris et approbatis conciliis ac constitutionibus et auctoritatibus summorum pontificum et sanctorum patrum ac consensu catholicae ecclesiae.'

[5] CT VII/I 375–377, 13.

recitation of the words of consecration, the plea for use of the vernacular in the celebration of mass, and the vituperation of masses celebrated in honour of saints. The second new article presents the reformers' odium for catholic ceremonial and their defence of evangelical simplicity in celebration of the sacrament.

Like the other practical matters presented at Bologna, and repeated at Trent, these new ones show a fundamental difference over the nature of the mass. Since the reformers emphasized that the eucharist, mass, or Lord's Supper, is a proclamation of the death of Christ, calling for the faith needed to approach communion, they saw the silent recitation of the words of consecration and the latin mass as violations of what had been instituted by Christ.[6] Catholic defenders, on their side, linked both with the sacerdotal and sacrificial character of the mass.

To the reformers, the honouring of saints in the mass looked like a protraction of the doctrine of merit, whereas to catholics this was part and parcel of communion in the body of Christ.[7] This question of celebrating masses in honour of the saints, of course, belongs in the broader context of the veneration of the saints. The Reformers themselves do not seem to have been quite sure whether this was a matter of discipline or of doctrine. At first, it appears, Luther and Melanchton took it as a matter of correcting abuses in the veneration of the saints, abuses that obscured the truth of true worship. Melanchton, however, then put it into the context of doctrinal teaching, and it is this

[6] For a presentation of evangelical teaching, together with the changes in the celebration of the eucharist effected by Luther, Zwingli and Calvin, cf. Yngve Brilioth, *Eucharistic Faith and Practice: Evangelical and Catholic* (London: SPCK 1930. Reprint 1965).

[7] For a discussion of this issue at the time of the Reformation and for an account of medieval practice, cf. Georg Kretschmar and René Laurentin, 'The Cult of the Saints', in *Confessing One Faith* ... 262–285.

mixture of the doctrinal and the practical which is reflected in article 21 of the *Confessio Augustana*.[8] There it is said that the remembrance of the saints is commended to the faithful, because of their faith and good works, but that intercession of the saints contradicts the unique mediatorship of Jesus Christ, 'who is the only highpriest, advocate, and intercessor before God'. If any intercession of the saints violates this doctrinal principle, celebrating mass in their honour seemed all the more atrocious.

The quarrel over ceremonial as opposed to evangelical simplicity reflects two more fundamental quarrels. The first has to do with the place of traditions in the church and in the development of its practices. While this was part of the issue of the relation between scripture and its traditional interpretation, when related to the practice of worship and sacrament it reflects the reformers' feeling that human traditions were quite likely to have obscured and thwarted the original evangelical reality. The second quarrel has to do with the place of scripture in the church and in the life of the faithful. In worship, it was important for the reformers that the Word of God be heard and proclaimed, but for the catholics of the time the people were much better instructed and educated through ceremonial and the sacraments stood on their own, apart from scriptural proclamation.

Finally, there is the combination in 1551 of articles on the mass with articles on the sacrament of order. This simply reflects the fact that belief in the mass as sacrifice went along with the doctrine on order which emphasised priesthood. The two, mass and priesthood, were taken to be necessary counterparts, equally challenged by the protestants in their own teaching and practice.

The close links between doctrinal positions and practice,

[8] Tappert, *The Book of Concord* 46f.

reflected in the collection of alleged errors, needs to be kept in mind in reading the debates of 1547 and 1551/52. Looking at them, it will first be shown how some of the speakers answered the immediate objections to the *ex opere operato* efficacy of the mass's application. As already remarked, however, this was not taken to be the central issue, and so in the second place it will be shown how the speakers isolated the issue of propitiatory sacrifice, within the general typology which they offered of sacrifices. Thirdly, the clear concentration on the act of the priest in consecrating and offering will be illustrated. Then, fourthly, it will be shown how all of this was related by the speakers to the sacrifice of the cross.

### Answering the Reformers' Accusations

As has been seen, the texts from reformation writings, which formed the basis for the articles collected for theological discussion and refutation, had to do directly with the alleged *ex opere operato* efficacy of offering mass for the remission of sins, both fault and punishment. At Bologna, Ioannes Consilii and Antonio Ricci took time in the course of their respective interventions to answer these objections. Ricci complained that the 'heretics' attributed much to catholic thought that was in fact quite alien to it. The opposition, he said, of the doctrine of efficacy to the doctrine of justification was quite false. By their teaching on the mass, catholics did not mean that its efficacy came from the work of those who offered, but attributed whatever benefits come from the mass to the *opus operatum* which is Christ working in us. Whatever is done by the priest in the mass is done *in persona Christi*, and so the whole work is his, not ours.[9] Moreover, neither grace nor remission of sins can be

[9] Antonius Ricius CT VI/2 467 11–17: 'Cum vero adversarii caecutientes insurgunt et dicunt ex Paulo hominem iustificari ex fide, quare non ex operato missae, ut dicimus nos catholici, respondemus, quod ipsi haeretici se figunt nobis multa, quae a nostra sententia sunt alienissima. Non enim dicimus quod

obtained without faith and good disposition on the part of the recipient, and there is nothing automatic in the idea of *ex opere operato* efficacy.[10] For his part, Consilii dismissed as liars those who said that catholics believed that the offering of the eucharist justified sinners without a good movement of the will on the part of those who received its fruits.[11]

In these answers, we see a clarification concerning the dispositions of sinners which excludes an automatic remission of sin. We also see the stress on the mass as the act of the priest, but this is explained as the act or work of Christ done through the priest, not as the priest's own, or as the church's own, meritorious work.

Similar answers to these difficulties were given at Trent in 1551 by Iodocus Ravesteyn, Franciscus Sonnius and Marianus Rocha. Ravesteyn dismissed as calumny the idea that the mass adds anything to what was already merited for sinners on the cross, or that it offers any satisfaction for sin beyond the satisfaction made by Christ.[12] Rocha took up a specific problem raised by Wolfgang Musculus, whom Rocha took as his chief interlocutory on all points in the debate. Musculus had proposed a kind of *reductio ad absurdum* of catholic practice, saying that once a person had benefited from a mass offered, there was no need to offer any more masses for this person, since all sin would be remited through this one mass.[13] Rocha replied to this that Musculus had a very wrong notion of the meaning of applying a

ex nostro opere operato quasi de se iustificemur, sed ex opere operato, quod est Christi operantis in nobis. Nec eucharistia est nostrum opus, immo protestatur fidelis sacerdos consecrans totum fuisse factum in persona Christi . . .'

[10] ibid., 468 42.

[11] Ioannes Consilii CT VI/2 528 4f.: '. . . si adversarii dicant nos docere, quod eucharistiae oblatio aliquando sine bono motu ex opere operato iustificet, mentiuntur impie'.

[12] Iodocus Ravesteyn Tiletanus CT VII/2 408 5–18.

[13] Marianus Rocha explains this argument of Musculus CT VII/2 475 27–32.

mass for a person. This was not an act whereby the priest could command God's grace, much less merit it, but an act of intercession addressed to God's mercy in virtue of the merits of Christ, who is offered in the mass.[14] In this reply, Rocha favoured that side of medieval theology which advocated an application *per modum suffragii* rather than *per modum satisfactionis*.

Sonnius made an interesting use of the term *ex opere operato*, which is quite faithful to the origins of the term in scholastic theology. First of all, he used it in the sense that grace is attributed to the performance of the rite as such, rather than to the merits of minister or recipient. But then he added that the rite has its efficacy because the *opus operatum* is Christ, who is offered in the mass, so that contrary to the view of opponents that in catholic thought it is the priest who merits, it is Christ who through the mass absolves sins and reconciles sinners to God.[15]

These replies to stated objections could no doubt remove any concerns about forgiving sin to the unrepentant, or to those who did not have faith in Christ. However, they also show the catholic emphasis on the act of the priest in applying satisfactions and merits, and on the importance of the rite itself as the means through which Christ works in the church. This could not dispel reformers' discomfort with the role of the priest and with the role of sacrament, as distinct from word.

## The Mass a Sacrifice of Propitiation

Rather than answering the protestant objections to the mode of

[14] CT VII/2 477 19–22: 'Non enim meremur, sed interpellamus seu rogamus Deum; ut pet victimam, per merita Christi, redemptoris nostri, quae in hoc sacrificio offerimus, velit nobis et aliis indulgere. Non habet sacerdos auctoritatem imerandi Deo, sed officium supplicandi et humiliter intercedendi. An vero exaudiatur vel ne, ipse penitus ignorat.'

[15] Franciscus Sonnius CT VII/2 401 40–402 5.

efficacy, most of the speakers at both sessions here considered set out to prove that the mass is a sacrifice of propitiation. In this, they distinguished it from a thanksgiving sacrifice, or from a spiritual sacrifice, which is the offering of prayers and good works done in faith in Jesus Christ. Their attitude was that the reformers reduced the mass to these latter kinds of sacrifice, which indeed had a part in the mass, but did not constitute the peculiar character of the mass as such, that is, as priestly act offered in the person or in the name of Christ. It is quite interesting that the speakers should have addressed this distinction of sacrifices, since reformation thought on the mass as a sacrifice of praise and thanksgiving was not listed among the articles attributed as errors to the heretics.[16] Together with arguments against what they saw as a reduction of the mass to thanksgiving, the theologians also took up the cudgels against other elements of evangelical thought, such as the eucharist's testamentary nature, and the opinions of Zwingli and Calvin, which were read as a reduction of the eucharist to an incitement to subjective remembrance of the cross. Central to all of this was the interpretation of key scriptural passages, especially Hebrews 9.12 and 10.12 on the once and for all offering of Christ, Malachi 1.10f on the sacrifice to be offered by the gentiles, the texts on Melchisedech as figure of Christ and of his offering, 1 Cor 10.14ff., on eating at the Lord's table, and of course the words of Christ in the institution narratives.[17]

In face of all possible explanations of the act of eucharistic celebration, several speakers enunciated the issue in clear terms which enable us to see how exactly it was understood and defended. For example, Hieronymus ab Oleastro reminded the conciliar Fathers that the controversy was not about whether or

[16] The distinction between sacrifice of thanksgiving and sacrifice of propitiation did turn up as question thirteen in the session of 1562.

[17] An excellent example of scriptural refutation and argumentation is found in the intervention of Nicolaus Grandis VII/2 447–456.

not the mass, as practised in catholic tradition, is offered as a sacrifice for the expiation of sins. That this was so was clear. Hence the point of controversy was whether or not it was right to do so. Indeed, he stated his position in terms which appear quite shocking today, using the language of two sacrifices, which was quite common at Bologna but which was avoided in later sessions of the Council, when the question was reshaped. Hieronymus set out to show from scripture and tradition that besides the sacrifice of Christ for sins offered on the cross, there is another sacrifice which is the mass, offered in memorial of this original sacrifice.[18] At the same session at Bologna, Ioannes Consilii added a factor which helps to clarify the true nature of the controversy, namely, by opposing the doctrine of sacrifice to the reformation teaching that Christ gave the eucharist to the church, not as sacrifice but as a testament and sacrament.[19] In these ways of phrasing the question, it is evident that what was being asked was whether the mass, a memorial of the cross, was itself a sacrifice offering satisfaction for sin and its expiation.

At Trent in 1551 there was a subtle rephrasing of the question, which put more accent on the sacramental character of the eucharist, that is, its sacramental relation to the sacrifice of the cross. This allowed speakers to address themselves more to the application of the cross through the sacramental sacrifice of the mass, i.e. one in which the offering of the cross is represented. At the same time, however, theologians still saw a controversy between themselves and the reformers over the propitiatory

---

[18] Hieronymus ab Oleastro CT VI/2 492 1–4: 'Non controvertitur an missa sit sacrifitium, sed an debeat esse missa aut aliud sacrifitium peccatorum expiativum praeter Christum.'

[19] Ioannes Consilii CT VI/2 507 24–26: '. . . Christi preciosissimum corpus non tantum sumitur, ut sacrilegi isti volunt, sed et ante consecretur, offertur et adoratur'. One here see the central point of consecration, on which hang both the sacrifice and eucharistic adoration, and therefore the whole piety of catholic tradition in that era.

nature of this offering, made in the mass.

Ioannes Gropper, whose writing influenced speakers at both the 1551 session and the previous one,[20] summed up the points of argument in a way which expressed the Council's interest very neatly. What, he said, had been put to question was whether or not the church has a visible sacrifice, sacrament of the invisible sacrifice, one that has been instituted by Christ, offered first by him and then given to the apostles to be perpetually offered by the church. Included in this notion of visible sacrifice is that it is propitiatory, as well as eucharistic (i.e. one of thanksgiving), and that it can be applied for others, including the dead who have departed this life placing their faith and confidence in this sacrament, and that it benefits the church in all necessities.[21] Gropper's statement of the question is inclusive of all the important points of controversy: the existence of a visible sacrifice made by the church, distinct from the internal and spiritual offerings of the faithful, the institution of this by Christ himself, and its offering for sin, affecting both the living and the dead. Important, however, in his way of stating the question, as distinct for example from Oleastro, is the accent given to the sacramental mode of offering and representation. How this affects other questions will appear later.

It is from within the typology of sacrifices offered by many speakers at both sessions that one sees what exactly they

[20] On Gropper's influence and positions at Trent, cf. Freudenberger, 'Der Benützung . . .' 589ff.

[21] Ioannes Gropper CT VII/2 442 20–26: '. . . Hoc tantum in quaestionem venit; an sit in ecclesia sit aliquod sacrificium visibile, quod sit invisibilis sacrificii sacramentum, institutum a Christo et ab eo primum oblatum et postea apostolo et ecclesiae commendatum, perpetua celebratione gerendum, propiciatorium simul et eucharisticum, applicabile pro aliis, etiam mortuis, qui, cum hinc decesserint, suam fidem et animos ad huiusmodi sacrificium alligaeunt, quodque praeterea quam maxime utile et fructuosum sit ad omnes alias ecclesiasticas necessitates sublevandas.' For a similar enunciation of the question, cf. Ravesteyn CT VII/2 409 35–41.

intended by a propitiatory sacrifice, and how it is different from other kinds of offering. First of all, there was some attempt to give a generic definition of sacrifice, of which propitiatory would be one of the species. This attempt is interesting in itself, because it reveals a way of looking at the church, its institutions, sacraments and sacrifice, which places it in continuity with the law of nature and the old law. Rather than constituting a break with the law of nature and the mosaic law, the law of the gospel was seen as their perfection, bringing to completion that which they prefigured.

The generic definition of sacrifice was drawn from the words *offering* and *consecration*, or some synonymous term. Thomas Maria Beccatelli,[22] Thomas de Sancto Marino,[23] Franciscus Salazar[24] and Gratianus Hervet,[25] were content with a definition that identifies sacrifice with *sacrum facere* or *Deo dedicare*. Others tried to include the meaning and purpose of sacrifice in the definition. Thus Ricardus of Vercelli[26] and Franciscus of Siena[27] said that to make holy or consecrate to God was an expression of God's dominion and humanity's subordination and obedience.

In drawing up a catalogue of sacrifices, speakers for the most part took their distinctions from the Old Testament. Three different divisions of sacrifice were offered by different theologians. One was a simple division between thanksgiving sacrifice and propitiatory sacrifice.[28] Another distinguished three sorts of sacrifice, namely, peace offerings, which are also offerings of praise, offerings made to have communion with

[22] CT VI/2 445 20.
[23] CT VI/2 475 20f.
[24] CT VI/2 581 25.
[25] CT VI/2 592 33f.
[26] CT VI/2 436 25–27.
[27] CT VI/2 499 22ff.
[28] Nicolaus Grandis CT VI/2 447 12–36: Thomas de Sancto Marino 475 22–25: Franciscus Senensis 500 7–11: Franciscus Cesena 576 1f.

God, and sacrifices offered for the remission of sins.[29] Finally, some made a distinction between sacrifice in the metaphorical sense, which takes in prayers, good works, penance and thanksgiving, and sacrifice in the true and proper sense, which is that made for the propitiation of sin.[30] In each case, the sacrifice of propitiation stands out as distinct from others and provided theologians with the category needed to describe the nature of the mass.

Within this category of sacrifice for sin, however, a further distinction was made by some, in order to provide for an explanation of how the fruits of the mass were to be applied. Ioannes Antonius Delphinus, in his intervention at Bologna, distinguished in the Old Testament between sacrifices of propitiation and sacrifices of satisfaction. The first is offered to effect reconciliation with God on behalf of those alienated by sin. The second is offered to make reparation for the offence of God's honour, and could even include a readiness on the part of the offerer to undergo the punishment due the sinner. This allowed for a proportion between the extent of the offence and the extent of punishment due or the satisfaction needed to restore offended honour. Delphinus explained that cross and mass are each both propitiatory (or reconciliatory) and satisfactory, but in different ways. The sacrifice of the cross reconciled sinners with God and offered to God's honour the debt due, through the sufferings that Christ endured vicariously for sinners. The mass is also reconciliatory, because it is an offering of Christ to God, but it is at the same time satisfactory, because it applies to sinners the satisfaction made by Christ on the cross. In this distinction, it is clear that application is made of

---

[29] Ricardus Vercellensis CT VI/2 437 3f.: Hieronymus Papinus Laudensis 545 20ff.

[30] Franciscus Salazar CT VI/2 582f.

satisfaction, but the reconciliatory purpose of the mass is, as it were, its constant.[31]

When they spoke to the question of the mass, the theologians at both sessions used the above distinctions to explain that it is distinctively propitiatory or satisfactory. It could certainly be said to include a sacrifice of praise and thanksgiving, or sacrifices in the metaphorical sense, such as the prayers and good works of the faithful which are spiritual offerings. The error of the reformers was to call the eucharist a sacrifice only in these latter senses, whereas to be a true and proper sacrifice it had to have propitiatory value.

A further note can be made here on terminology. No clear distinction was made at Trent between propitiation and expiation, except by Delphinus, who equated propitiation with reconciliation, as seen, and used satisfaction and expiation as synonyms. Other spekers simply used propitiation or expiation indiscriminately, even when they made a distinction between the remission of sin and the remission of punishment due to sin. The major argument against the reformers made the point that the mass is offered for the 'remission of sins' in a general way, and this meant that it is dubbed a sacrifice of propitiation, or in some cases a sacrifice of expiation. It was on particulars that speakers showed no common approach, especially when they had to explain what exactly is remitted by the mass's offering, or how the mass works, that is, as suffrage or as satisfaction.

### The Act of the Priest

The Tridentine theologians and bishops could agree with Melanchton or any other reformer, when he said that the celebration of the mass included sacrifices of thanksgiving and spiritual sacrifices. However, to confine oneself to this was felt by them to be deficient on two counts. First of all, as already

---

[31] Ioannes Antonius Delphinus CT VI/2 606f.

64

said, it left out that which is most distinctive of the mass, propitiation. Secondly, and this was intimately related to the first point, Melanchton was talking about the acts of all the faithful, the things done during the mass or in conjunction with it, whereas for the Tridentine speakers the theology of sacrifice suited to the mass was a theology that concerned the specific act of the priest-celebrant, when he consecrated the bread and wine and offered the gift consecrated. In some cases, the speaker included the offering in the very act of consecration,[32] in others he distinguished the two, placing the offering or oblation immediately after the consecration, as expressed in the words of the Roman canon.[33] In either case, the act of the priest as priest was distinguished from all else that occurred in the mass. Indeed, the whole dispensation of the mass, including its application and the system of private masses, seemed to stand or fall on the explanations given of this act. Like the theology of the eucharist as sacrament, so too the theology of the mass as sacrifice espoused at the Council of Trent was a theology of the power and act of the ordained priest.

The arguments given for the use of the private mass, for the silent recitation of the words of consecration, or for the use of latin, all reveal the notion that the mass as such was the affair of the priest, a holy thing into which he alone entered. He was indeed taken to act as minister of the church and for the people in what he did, but the people were not deemed to have any direct part of his actions. In arguing for the private mass, it was said that this practice dates back to earliest tradition, support

[32] This does not appear to have been a common position, but *may be* that taken by Nicolaus Grandis (CT VI/2 451 32–452 23) and Alexander de Bononia (CT VI/2 459 25–37) who both, in speaking of the parts of the mass, find the essential elements in the words of consecration and make no mention of a distinct oblation, as other speakers do, when they list as essential consecration, oblation and communion.

[33] The words of the canon 'Unde et memores offerimus ...' are the evidence.

being adduced even from the Pseudo-Dionysius, who of course was taken at that time to be the Areopagite known from the Acts of the Apostles, contemporary therefore to the apostles and a good witness to the doings of the apostolic age.[34] Others argued that in instituting the mass, Christ gave no instructions about the communion of the faithful, the supposition being that only the apostles were present at the Supper to receive the Lord's Body and Blood and that on that occasion they were ordained priests. Hence it was left to priests, in the person of the apostles who received the command to offer and to take, eat and drink, to decide how the communion of the faithful was to be regulated.[35] Many speakers acknowledged that in early christian times communion was frequent and a regular part of celebration, but they deemed later conciliar rulings about less frequent communion quite appropriate and within the power of church authority, answering to the less fervent condition of the age. Indeed, on the subject of private mass one theologian found that a mass literally celebrated in private could be of more benefit to the church than one said in public, since when not surrounded by a distracting populace the priest could celebrate more devoutly.[36] Comparable arguments were adduced in favour of the silent consecration (or even canon) and of the use of latin, both practices being viewed as conducive to the sense of

[34] Franciscus a Conceptione (CT VI/2 554f.) and Hieronymus ab Oleastro (CT VI/2 496 6–21) both remark on the presence in the Supper room of the apostles alone. Hence they argue that as Christ himself did not expect all the christians in Jerusalem at the time to come to the mass, the church is free to have masses where only the priest celebrates. Arguments from tradition can have an amusing side, as in the case of Ioannes Mahusius who dated the tradition of mixing water with wine back to Christ on the basis of his sobriety and asceticism, an asceticism so great that at age thirty-three he was taken to be nearly fifty, as we read in John 8.57 (CT VII/2 426 20).

[35] E.g., Petrus Paulus Iannarinus CT VI/2 564 4–6: Ruardus Tapper CT VII/2 376 44–377 5: Ioannes Orthega CT VII/2 389 22, who says that the *spectatores missae* do not have to receive communion.

[36] Tapper CT VII/2 377 9–16.

awe and mystery that should appropriately surround the action of the priest when he offered sacrifice.[37]

Quite interestingly, it was in reference to the act of the priest performed in reciting the words of institution that some efforts were made in the 1551/52 session to find a way of joining together the eucharistic and the propitiatory aspects of the sacrifice. Many of the speakers simply placed the sacrifice of thanksgiving before the sacrifice proper, identifying it with the preface of the canon or some other parts of the mass. A few, however, expressed the view that the act of the priest in or after the consecration was at one and the same time an act of thanksgiving and an act of propitiation. In other words, the priest was said to offer Christ in thanksgiving and propitiation at one and the same time. Ruardus Tapper developed his understanding of the priestly act in this manner, by using the definition of Augustine in *The City of God*, Bk 10, chapter 6, that a sacrifice is every good work by which we enter into communion with God.[38] The good work for him includes thanks and satisfaction. In the case of those present who receive communion, the communion in the sacrifice is obtained in this way. When the mass is offered without communicants, or for the absent, the communion is obtained through the propitiatory side of the act, since such persons receive a communion in God's good through the effects of propitiation, even if they cannot join in the ends of thanksgiving, not being present in person.[39]

Others who combined thanksgiving and propitiation in the one act of offering were Orthega, Sonnius and the Jesuit, Lainez, for whom the body and blood of the Lord made present through the consecration were then offered by the priest in

[37] E.g., Bartholamaeus Carranza de Miranda CT VII/2 529f.: Ravesteyn VII/2 414: Orthega CT VII/2 390 12–33.

[38] CT VII/2 372 18f. The text quoted from Augustine reads: 'Opus, quod agebatur, ut sancta societate inhaereamus Deo'.

[39] 372 25–41.

thanksgiving and propitiation.[40] Sonnius added a particular note of his own, saying that the fraction was part of the rite of offering. This, however, was just a way of following up on the argument for the institution of the sacrifice from the words about breaking the bread in the supper narrative.[41]

Not only the theologians, but also the bishops, when their turn came to speak, concentrated on the act of the priest when they argued for a propitiatory sacrifice. Few made the point more clearly than Julius Pflug, Bishop of Naumburg, in the 1551/52 session. Rather irenically (for he was more interested in the possibilities of reconciliation than most of the others, who took defence and aggression as their key-note) he noted that the spiritual sacrifice of the faithful was indeed more important than the sacramental sacrifice of the priest, since without it no fruits could be gathered.[42] However, in discussing the application of fruits, he made it clear that this was done by his ministerial act as such. This Pflug called the priest's *nudum ministerium*, the precise act in which the sacrifice of Christ is represented and nothing of the priest himself or of the church enters into account.

One of the scripture texts that received much attention in the interventions was Mal 1.10f., where the prophet foretold the sacrifice that was to replace the legal sacrifices and to be offered by the gentiles from the rising of the sun to its setting. This text had often been used in tradition in writing of the eucharist. Reformers and catholics alike agreed that it could be taken as a eucharistic text. For the reformers, however, it meant the prayers and good works of the faithful joined with the

[40] Iacobus Lainez CT VII/2 531 39–532 1: Ioannes Orthega VII/2 386f.: Franciscus Sonnius VII/2 397 32ff.

[41] Arguments for the institution of a sacrifice at the Supper were largely drawn from an analysis of certain terms, such as doing (*facite* was said to belong to a sacrificial vocabulary and certainly to mean something more than receiving a sacrament), breaking, giving, pouring out, as well as from the actions of Jesus, in blessing, raising his eyes to heaven, and breaking the bread.

[42] Julius Pflug CT VII/2 628 29–33.

celebration of the sacrament, and the thanksgiving prayers that were part of the ceremony. The Tridentine speakers, for their part, attached the words of the prophet to the propitiatory sacrifice offered by the priest. In this way, the use of the text in two different meanings pin-pointed the exact nature of what was under dispute.

## The Mass and the Cross

The speakers at the two sessions of the synod referred to objections drawn by the reformers against the sacrifice of the mass from Hebrews 9.12 and 10.12. They wished to answer the difficulty that the mass if considered as sacrifice takes away from the once-for-all efficacy of the sacrifice of the cross and from the unique mediatorship of Jesus Christ. At Bologna in 1547, this was largely a matter of explaining that, though itself a sacrifice, the mass was a memorial sacrifice, in which the victim offered was Christ himself made sacramentally present, and not something new. In 1551, the theologians often took a different approach, explaining how the mass as representative sacrifice applied the fruits of the cross.

Before going into detailed explanation of these arguments, a preliminary of the way in which redemption was understood is appropriate. It was certainly not the intention of the speakers to explain how the redemption is effected through the cross of Christ, but certain assumptions about this affected the way of explaining the mass. As one might expect, the most basic assumption was that the cross itself was a sacrifice of propitiation for sin, in which Christ reconciled the world with the Father, made satisfaction for sin, and merited grace for humanity. Satisfaction and merit were the categories that determined both soteriology and eucharistic doctrine. Franciscus of Siena quoted Melanchton's definition of propitiatory sacrifice as one on which they would both agree and which they would both apply to the cross: it is nothing other than that work which makes satisfaction for sins, reconciles us to God the Father, and placates God's anger.[43] Though this definition mentions the placation of God's anger and the offering of satisfaction for injury done, it does not follow that the image of a God of strict justice or of an angry God dominated the discussion and the suppositions about the redemption. On the contrary, some of the interventions follow out a line of thought found in Thomas Aquinas, which wed the category of satisfaction with love.[44] It is more because of his love that Christ is said to have made satisfaction for sin than for reasons of a penalty that had to be paid.[45] Nonetheless, the discussion of the mass as representation and application of the cross could not be extricated from the categories of merit and satisfaction, nor from the quantitative connotations of the latter. The same thing has to be said of the discussion at Trent in 1551, where Antonius Marinarius, referred to by the Wittemberg theologians who observed the debate, taking copious notes, as 'a monk dressed in black', disabused his audience of what he took to be Luther's understanding of the cross. It was not, he said, because of the pain which he suffered that Christ redeemed us, but because of the great charity and obedience that he displayed. Nonetheless, in explaining his ideas further, Antonius returned to the categories of merit and placation.[46]

---

[43] CT VI/2 500 7f.: '. . . nihil aliud est quam opus pro peccatis satisfactorium nosque Deo reconcilians iramque Dei placans'.

[44] Cf. S. Th. III, q. 48, art. 2, c.

[45] Ricardus Vercellensis VI/2 437 36–38: '. . . et obtulit seipsum pro nobis magna charitate, ut placaret patrem. Et hoc ipsum opus, quod voluntarie passionem sustinuit, Deo maxime acceptum fuit, utpote ex charitate proveniens, et sic passio Christ fuit verum sacrificium.' Compare Nicolaus Grandis 448 24f.: 'Sed oblatio Christi verum est sacrificium, Eph. 5.2: Dilexit nos et tradidit semetipsum hostiam et oblationem in odore suavitatis'.

[46] CT VII/2 492–509 and 576–580, the latter passage being the notes of the Wittemberg scholars. Some of the speakers got short shrift from this pair, who, for example, after a few brief notes account for the inquisitor Gregorius Sylvius by remarking that he spoke at length with a vehemence and bitterness such that words could not express (CT VII/2 560 25). In his notes, the Council

The words *representation* and *commemoration* were key ones in explaining the relation of the mass to the cross, but they could be understood in a number of different ways, the only common thing being that they did not mean subjective recall of Christ's passion, which was said to be the idea of Calvin or Zwingli. Two theologians at Bologna explored this vocabulary more deeply. Ioannes Consilii in his reading of the supper narrative gave an erudite explanation of the greek word *anamnesis*. He argued from Aristotle, Plato and Ammonius that the word meant not only the recall of a thing once known but a true renewal and representation of what is remembered.[47] Ricardus of Vercelli expressed the relationship of the mass to the cross as that of a *perfecta imago*, comparing it to the way in which Christ is the perfect image of God.[48] Cross and mass differ from one another only in the *modus essendi*: the cross was a bloody act, whereas the mass represents it in an unbloody way, as befits the relation of image to that which it represents.

However, when the two theologians went on to explain the nature of the relationship they pressed only the identity of what is offered in either case. There was no question for them of an identity of offering, as if the original act of offering were sacramentally present in the mass. The language of image and representation was applied to the victim, in one way, to the offering in another. The victim, Jesus Christ, is present in the

secretary Massarelli gave the same gentleman only a few lines. For all then that remains of his intervention, one could say that he was blowing into the wind.

[47] CT VI/2 513 30–42, especially the words: 'Haec quippe (ie. *eis ten emen anamnesin*) non simpliciter significat commemorationem aut memoriam, sed quandam praeteritae scientiae aut rei scitae renovationem repraesentationemque.'

[48] CT VI/2 437 41–46: 'Quando unum est perfecta imago alterius, quicquid convenit uni, convenit alteri. Et quia filius in divinis est perfecta imago patris ... ideo omnia attributa patris conveniunt filio. Sed eucharistia est perfecta imago Christi crucifixi, quum sit non solum similis in specie, sed idem Christus, differens solum quoad modum essendi.'

same identity in both sacrifices, but in the mass he is presented in sacrament or image. The offering of the cross is not present in its own identity, but in another offering, which is its image. Ricardus spoke about the *idem Christus*, not about the *eadem passio*. It is as crucified that Christ is imaged and present in the mass. There is, in fact, some ambiguity in the way that Ricardus explained himself, as if he were working out a solution, not giving one that was standard. In one instance, he said that it is the crucified Christ who is imaged,[49] in another that it is the passion and that it is the passion which the priest offers.[50] The key to his thought, however, seems to lie in the fact that he placed the oblation *after* the consecration, so that when the priest offers it is the crucified Christ who is offered.[51] Ioannes Consilii also, despite his elucidations on *anamnesis*, separated consecration and oblation, so that he could put the identity of the two acts in the offering of the one victim. In fact, he related the reformers' problems as problems that had to do with a succession of victims, not with a succession of offerings.[52]

For the Bologna theologians, the very reason for having the sacrifice of the mass lay in the need to have a means, other than the sacraments, which applies to particular individuals the

[49] ut supra.

[50] ibid., 439 32f.: 'Obiectum autem missae est passio Christi, quam offert sacerdos et repraesentat celebrans missam'.

[51] ibid., 440 5: '... post consecrationem offertur ipse Christus et sanctissima eius passio ...'. The ambiguity shows still further in that immediately preceding these words, Ricardus had listed the four parts of the mass as doctrine, consecration, communion and prayer, making no specific mention of oblation.

[52] CT VI/2 514 25–27: '... hostiam, quam obtulit Christus et quam nos quotidie offerimus, unam eandemque esse, nempe verum corpus et sanguinem Christi, et vanam falsamque esse istius modi hostiarum successionem ab istis conflictam et nobis obiectam.' Consilii had already intervened at length in the session of the Council on the sacrament of the eucharist on the presence of Christ, and it is this presence which was for him the key to the question of sacrifice.

merits and satisfactions of the cross. The victim offered in both cases is the same. In instituting the mass, Christ also instituted the priesthood, and in offering the mass the priest acts as a minister of Christ and as a minister of the church. This left room to distinguish between the offerer of the cross and the offerer of the mass. The priest was said to act in the power of Christ, because of the institution of the priesthood by him, but the offerer whom he was thought to represent was the church. This distinction of offerers opened the way to explain the limited fruits of the mass, as distinct from the unlimited fruits of the cross.

The fact that the priest receives his power from Christ was enough to warrant the assertion that he acts *vice Christi* or *in persona Christi*. These expressions could be given a strong sense in respect of the consecration, for it is Christ himself who through the priest transforms the bread and wine into his body and blood. In respect of the offering, they have a weaker sense, for then it is enough to say that the priest has the power to make the church's offering and the application of fruits from Christ. The matter, as can be seen, is quite tangled. Christ operates the consecration through the priest and operates the effects of grace, but the church makes the offering of the victim, and this explains the limits of its fruits.

Some examples of this way of reasoning need to be quoted. Thomas de Sancto Marino distinguished between the offerer of the mass and the offerer on the cross, but explained that the power to offer on behalf of the church is a divine power given by Christ, and so can be the medium for transmitting grace and the remission of sins.[53] It was in answer to the objection that the

---

[53] CT VI/2 477 12–17: 'Respondetur quod ecclesia non offert Christum eo modo, quo semel in cruce oblatus est. Nec ascribit oblationi suae servitutis remissionem peccatorum. Nec applicat hanc ut opus meritorium remissionis culpae et penae. Sed praenuntiat se hanc oblationem offerre in memoriam passionis, resurrectionis et ascensionis Yhesu Christi. Et petit sibi applicari per

malice of the priest might affect the outcome of the offering, that Alexander de Bononia explained his thought. In the mass, he said, there are two offerers, the principal one which is the church, and the priest who is its minister. It is the devotion of the principal offerer which determines the quantity of fruit dispensed. Here, he fell back on the medieval explanations already quoted, taking the church as a social body, whose devotion is corporately determined and varies from day to day.[54]

Ioannes Delphinus in his elaborations on application made the distinctions very clearly. The fruit of the mass, he explained, comes neither from the church nor from the priest, but from Christ, who is the *opus operatum* of the mass, the victim that is offered. Of this victim, there are two offerers, the church and its minister, the priest. Because both victim and offerer are pleasing to God, the mass obtains fruits for those for whom it is applied, not according to the measure of the victims but according to the measure of the offerer's devotion. To the limitation coming from the offerer, there is added the limitation coming from the side of the beneficiary, for not all beneficiaries are equally disposed in faith and will to receive grace and remission of sins.[55]

At Trent in 1551, the theologian who came closest to the positions taken at Bologna was Ioannes Orthega.[56] Though he said that it was Christ who works *ex opere operato* through the

---

fidem fructum oblationis Christi.' Another speaker, Antonius Ricius, very explicitly excluded an offering by Christ himself in the mass, CT VI/2 469 36ff: 'In hac (crucis) sese obtulit Deo patri in sacrificium . . . In hoc (missae) non sese offert: offertur autem a sacerdote in persona ecclesiae. In illa meritum fuit infinitum: in ista limitatum ex parte offerentis.'

[54] CT VI/2 459 4–15.

[55] CT VI/2 608–613. His position could be summed up in the sentence: 'Bonum, quod in eucharistia certis personis applicatur, est ipse Christus ut oblatus a persona, quae est grata et accepta Deo ratione voluntatis ecclesiae universalis.'

[56] Ioannes Orthega CT VII/2 388 32–41.

mass in conferring remission of sin and grace, he attributed limitation of the fruits received to the devotion of the priest-celebrant. Somehow, the priest's impetration came as an intermediary between Christ and the recipient of grace. In general, however, one can note a different turn in the way in which the relation of mass and cross was considered at this session.

To be sure, in using the language of commemoration and representation at the 1551 session theologians continued to put primary emphasis on the identity of the victim. When Franciscus Sonnius said that the mass was a commemorative and symbolic offering, he explained that this was because of the presence of the same victim in both offerings.[57] However, there seemed to be more interest in trying to explain the representative presence of the passion or death. Thus Carranza de Miranda making the point that the host offered in the mass is the same as on the Cross, adds that the mass is representative image of the passion.[58] Melchior Cano said that the mass shows forth the death of Christ in such a way that the immolated Christ is, as it were (*ac si*) present. This means that when Christ is offered, he is offered as having died.[59] In this, as Iserloh has

[57] Sonnius repeated the idea that it is necessary to have the mass, because of the very universality of the cross, but he calls it a symbolic oblation: '. . . Colligere licet et Christum obtulisse in cena et determinationes illas pro vobis et pro multis referendas esse ad oblationem symbolicam sub speciebus panis et vini, non ad oblationem factam in cruce quoniam certum est illam factam esse pro omnibus omnium aetatum omniumque aetatum hominibus . . .' (CT VII/2 399 33–36). What he argues here is that the supper and the mass are the symbolic representation of the offering of the cross, carried over into heaven, and that this symbolic offering is of its nature and intent restricted in its beneficiaries, something that was true already at the supper, when Christ offered only for the apostles who were present, whereas on the cross he offered himself for all.

[58] CT VII/2 521 38–522 4.

[59] CT VII/1: 'Nos offerimus Christum, quantus pro nobis mortuus est, et illam mortem exhibemus; et offerimus Christum ea ratione, qua mortuus est, non quatenus vivit. Et est, ac si praesens esset.' There is no written *votum* from

noted, there seems to have been an influence of Cajetan on a number of the speakers at the 1551/52 session.[60] This influence appears in an even more interesting way in a few speakers who tried to explain the relation of the offering, and not only of the victim, in the mass to the cross by way of the relation to the last supper and to Christ's heavenly intercession.

## The Mass, the Supper and Christ's Heavenly Priesthood

Trying to explain how the mass is representation and application of the sacrifice of the cross, led three speakers among the theologians at the 1551/52 session of the Council to bring the offering of Christ made at the last supper and his heavenly priesthood into the equation. These were Ruard Tapper, Ioannes Gropper and Franciscus Sonnius. They did not really succeed in resolving all the problems about application, but at least they did bring into consideration certain elements which took on considerable importance in the final synodal session of 1562.

Most of the speakers at Bologna and Trent seemed to assume that Christ had offered a sacrifice at the supper, since their arguments for the sacrificial nature of the eucharist were drawn from the words of Christ and implied that he had himself made an offering at the supper. Christ commanded the apostles to do as he had done, saying *Hoc facite*. The verb *facere* was given a sacrificial meaning by the theologians, so that the command to do as he had *done* meant that he had himself sacrificed his body and blood under the forms of bread and wine. The latin words

Melchior Cano in the *Acta*, but only the notes of Massarelli and the Wittemberg observers.

[60] Iserloh, 'Das Tridentinische Messopferdekret . . .', notes the influence of Cajetan on Bishop Friederich Nausea of Vienna, and on the theologians, Tapper, Ravesteyn, Gropper, Eberhard Billick and Ambrosius Pelargus. Of Cajetan's position, he writes: 'Christus wird nach Cajetan nicht gegenwärtig, um denn von uns geopfert zu werden, sondern er ist in der Weise des Opfers gegenwärtig (*Immolatitio modo*)' (p. 409f.).

*datur, effunditur, frangitur* were all called into evidence, since they were taken to be sacrificial terms and in the vulgate occurred in the present tense, nobody worrying too much about possible differences between the greek and the latin.[61]

On this common basis, Franciscus Sonnius built up a theory connecting supper, cross and mass, saying that in all three there is but one oblation, begun in the supper, completed on the cross, eternally enduring in heaven, and now sacramentally represented in the mass.[62] It was the relation of the mass to the heavenly oblation that Ruard Tapper developed, having already argued for an offering at the supper from the fact that Christ there took on a new *esse sacramentale* by making his body and blood present in the form of bread and wine. It was this offering, according to Tapper, that showed him to be a priest according to the order of Melchisedech, and it was according to this priesthood that he entered through the shedding of his blood on the cross into the eternal priesthood of heaven, where he makes continual intercession for humanity. He argued from the texts Hebrews 9.24 and Psalm 109.4, and concluded that the mass, as commemoration of the cross, is one with the heavenly intercession, which in turn began with the entry into the sanctuary through the shedding of blood.[63] In brief, for Tapper the assumption of a sacramental being by Christ at the supper and in the mass constitutes a propitiatory but sacramental offering, which is a commemoration of the cross and a sacramental representation of the enduring offering of Christ in heaven.

---

[61] For opinions at this session favourable to an offering at the supper, cf. Lainez CT VII/2 531 39–532 1: Tapper 372 22–24: Arze 542 7ff.: Sonnius 397 32–40: Mahusius 419f.: Ambrosius Pelargus 555 19–556 23: Delphius 557 8–14: Carranza de Miranda 527 28–528 33: Gropper 446 46f.: de Castro 539 18–42.

[62] CT VII/2 395 20–29.

[63] CT VII/2 373 41–374 24.

How did all of this affect the problems about the application of the fruits of the cross through the mass? Tapper's efforts on this point do not look wholly successful. Though he emphasised the intercessory character of Christ's eternal priesthood, he held on to a distinction between remission through an *ex opere operato* efficacy and an efficacy through the mode of impetration, as well as to a distinction between the remission of sin and the remission of pain through satisfaction rendered. The analogue for *ex opere operato* efficacy in the mass is the sacrament, and for Tapper the remission of punishment, for those properly disposed, works *ex opere operato* in a way comparable to the giving of grace through the sacraments. He professed himself unsure about the way in which the mass remits fault or sin, both venial and mortal. Since he believed the sacrament of penance necessary for those in mortal sin, it was clear that the offering of the mass for them would not work without at least a *votum sacramenti*. Given this point, he was prepared to admit that the mass remits sin *ex opere operato*, as in the sacraments, but he refrained from pushing this point. As for other spiritual benefits, and for temporal ones, these he believed to be given in answer to impetration, not *ex opere operato*, understood that the prayer made or offered is the heavenly prayer of Christ.[64]

Gropper followed much the same line of thought, with some modifications. He used the Augustinian definition *visibilis forma invisibilis sacrificii* to argue his points, making the mass the visible form of the offering begun by Christ on the cross and continuing in heaven.[65] He explained the efficacy of the mass in the distribution of fruits in much the same way as Tapper, but he

[64] CT VII/2 376 2–34.

[65] CT VII/2 443 14–16: '. . . missa visibilis sit invisibilis oblationis Christi olim in cruce et inde semper sine intermissione in sempiterno suo sacerdotio patri coelesti se pro nobis sistentis et delicta nostra repropriciantis visibilis forma.' Cf. also Franciscus Condelmerius VII/2 479 37–47, according to whom Christ pleads in heaven that the offering of the mass may be acceptable to God.

differed from him in putting some limit on the fruits at the door of the priest-celebrant. Since to the *opus Christi* there is added the *opus sacerdotis*, satisfaction and merit are meted out, not through the merit of the priest, but in proportion to his devotion and intention.[66] Another interesting point peculiar to Gropper is that he was careful not to separate the fruits of the mass totally from the fruits of sacramental communion, and required a *votum sacramenti* as one of the dispositions needed in those receiving the fruits of the mass. This he extended even to the case of dead beneficiaries, for it was only to those who carried this desire with them into purgatory that remission of punishment could be given.[67]

The most important point in these interventions is that they were able to get away from the idea that the mass may be a distinct offering from that of the cross by using the idea of sacramental representation more rigorously and by appealing to the connection between the cross and Christ's heavenly priesthood.[68] The true nature of sixteenth century dilemmas, however, also shows up in them, since despite this basic sacramental principle the speakers still had to tackle the issue of application in terms of merit and satisfaction. The sacramental principle could explain the connection between mass and cross for them, by the inclusion of the cross's heavenly continuance, but it could not explain for them the propitiatory role of the mass, since that required talk of satisfaction, merit and redemption from punishment as well as from sin. To attribute all effects to Christ's intercession sacramentally represented would not have sufficed in their minds, for that would have meant an abandonment of the *ex opere operato* principle.

[66] CT VII/2 445 23–447 4.

[67] l.c.

[68] One should be careful not to conclude that the conciliar decree intended this meaning. As will be seen, it was written in such a way as to leave the nature of the offering in the mass open to several interpretations.

*Application of the Fruits of the Mass*

The possibility of the priest's offering the mass for the living and the dead was essential to what was understood by the propitiatory nature of the sacrifice of the mass. It was important for the theologians to show that this was a practice from earliest times in the church. Besides, therefore, quoting papal and conciliar authorities from more recent times, they offered a florilegium of patristic texts, most of them intended to prove that the mass could be offered even for the dead and that it had been so offered. As for so many other practices, the Pseudo-Dionysius was quoted as an important witness, since the speakers believed this is to be indeed the Areopagite mentioned in the Acts of the Apostles.[69] Other frequent patristic texts quoted were: Tertullian, *De Corona Militis* 3.3;[70] Cyprian, *Ep.* 1.2;[71] Augustine, *Confessions* IX, 12 and *De Civitate Dei* XX, 9;[72] John Chrysostom, *In 1 Cor.* 41.4 and *In Matt.* 25.3 and *In Phil.* 3.4.[73] The meaning of such texts and the practices which they indicate will be discussed later in this work. For the moment, it is enough to say that as used at the Council they are a good example of its typical proof-text usage. The theory was there before the texts were offered and they were offered without close examination, as corroboration of a practice to be defended against the reformers.

In explaining the way in which the mass benefits those for

[69] Cited by Ricardus Vercellensis CT VI/1 326 27f.: Iacobus Lainez CT VII/1 382: Franciscus Sonnius CT VII/1 395.

[70] Cited by Sonnius l.c.: Delphinus CT VII/1 427.

[71] Cited by Riccardus Cenomanus CT VI/1 338 28–339 4: Sonnius l.c.: Antonius Marinarius CT VII/1 429.

[72] Cited by Nicolaus Grandis CT VI/1 331 7–12: Riccardus Cenomanus l.c.: Ioannes Consilii CT VI/1 350 38f.: Petrus Paulus Iannarinus CT VI/1 363 5–9: Sonnius l.c.: Marinarius l.c.

[73] Cited by Nicolaus Grandis, Riccardus Cenomanus, Lainez, Sonnius, Delphinus, Marinarius, l.c.

whom the priest offers it, the theologians found the distinction between making satisfaction for sin and obtaining remission of the sin itself an important one. At times, however, they found applying the distinction quite complicated. It was a relatively simple matter to attribute *ex opere operato* efficacy to the payment of satisfaction for one whose sins were already forgiven. Since the notion had a quantitative ring to it, measuring it out by way of an intentional application seemed understandable. Remission of sin itself, especially mortal, as a fruit of the mass was less easy to account for, both because it raised the issue of proper disposition in a more serious way and because it depended on divine mercy, not upon a dispensation which seemed to be by divine ordinance in the hands of the church. The authority of the church in meting out and commuting satisfactions, and its power in forgiving sins, were not taken to be identical.

Ioannes Delphinus dealt with this through the distinction between propitiation or reconciliation and satisfaction or expiation, when he gave his address at Bologna.[74] As a prayer and intercession of the church, according to him, the mass might obtain grace for the sinner from the divine mercy. On the other hand, the church could apply the merit and satisfaction of Christ directly to the remission of punishment, and even to the remission of venial sin, for even in this case the person did not need to be reconciled to God.

More was said at the 1551 Tridentine session than at Bologna on the application of the mass. A considerable difference of opinion on modalities was registered. The one common opinion was that the church through the offering and application of the mass could remit punishment for sin, through an application of the satisfaction of the cross. Beyond this, some thought that it could have nothing whatever to do with the

[74] CT VI/2 608–613.

remission of mortal sin.[75] Others were of the opinion that as an act of impetration, pleading the merits of Christ, it could obtain the grace of repentance, even for very serious sins. On the question of venial sins, generally speaking the theologians included its remission among the fruits of the mass, but the point of discussion was whether this came about *ex opere operato* or as a result of intercession, that is, whether it was *per modum satisfactionis* or *per modum suffragii*.

In addressing themselves to the power of the mass as intercession, as distinct from satisfaction, the speakers did not always keep a clear distinction between the efficacy of the general prayers of the mass rite and the precise sacerdotal act of the minister, which in other parts of their discourse they dubbed the sacrifice of propitiation. Hence, when it came to the turn of the bishops to address the assembly, Julius Pflug, referring as already said to the *nudum ministerium* of the priest, asked that the Council be clearer on what came about as a result of the general prayers of priest and people, and what was attributable to the application of the priestly act of sacrifice.[76]

*Presentation of Doctrine to the Bishop, 3rd January 1552*
As is well known, the theologians' elaborations at Bologna were without issue. The pope and emperor continued to disagree over the place, composition and purpose of the Council. The conciliar machinery made its sluggish way to Trent in the course of these disagreements, but there the synod drew to a halt and the matter of the mass was left in abeyance.

In 1551, the theologians completed their work by composing a doctrinal statement, divided into four chapters, which was then given to the conciliar fathers for their discussion and scrutiny. This doctrine was presented in plenary session on the

[75] Cf. Melchior Canon CT VII/1 389 2–390 19: Franciscus Sonnius CT VII/2 401 24–402 3.
[76] CT VII/2 629 13–630 35.

3rd of January, 1552, and on the following day some censures on the heretical articles that had been discussed by the theologians were suggested.

Apparently, there is only one extant manuscript of these chapters. The Societas Goerresiana in its publication of the *Acta* does not give a separate presentation of this doctrine, but indicates by way of foot-note where the original content differed from the revised version, presented later in the month.[77] In this way, it is made possible to compare the early version with the revised version, which came after the bishops' interventions.

In the doctrine as presented in early January, the first chapter explained that the mass, as offered by priests, is a true and proper sacrifice. To call it a sacrifice is then not simply a metaphorical usage. From the debate, it seems clear that this was meant to eliminate the idea that the mass is a subjective commemoration of the passion, or that it is just the sacrifice of thanksgiving of which the reformers spoke, or the sacrifice of obedience made by the faithful. The chapter then went on to state that the mass is a commemoration and sign of the sacrifice of the cross, instituted by Christ to be offered by priests. This was an answer to the charge that the mass adds to the merits of Christ, while at the same time being an affirmation of a visible sacrifice and a visible priesthood. In contrasting the sacrifice of the cross with the sacrifice of the mass, instituted at the supper, the chapter described the cross as a fulfilment of the priesthood of Aaron and the mass as a fulfilment of the priesthood of Melchisedech. At this stage, then, the language of two sacrifices and two

---

[77] CT VII/1 475–483. Compare the text given there with the foot-notes, which refer to the original version of the 3rd January. For a summary of this doctrine, cf. H. Jedin, *Geschichte* . . . Bd. III 354f. On p. 524, note 26, Jedin mentions that Franciscus Nausea, Bishop of Vienna, attributed the composition of the text to the theologians Lippmani, Tapper, Carranza de Miranda, Cano, Ilave, Gropper and Billick. Jedin himself suspects that Lainez had a hand in it, because of similarities with his *votum*.

priesthoods was still used, but, as will be seen, this was not well received by the bishops.

The second chapter presented the reasons why, over and above the sacraments, the church needs the sacrifice as means of grace. The repercussions of the debate are clear. The sin-offering of the cross, it is said, made once and for all for the sins of the whole world, brings remission of sin and grace through baptism. For sins committed after baptism, another means that would open the way to penance for sin, and satisfaction for punishment incurred, is necessary. This is the sacrifice of the mass, whose *vis* and *efficacia* come from the cross, by the offering of the same Christ in a different way. This is also dangerously close to the language of two sacrifices.

In the third chapter, the application of the mass was explained. First of all its relation to the cross is affirmed, for the mass's acceptability as an offering derives from the fact that *in mysterio* it shows forth the bloody death of Christ, there being no forgiveness without the shedding of blood. The mass is of such efficacy that it can obtain the remission of sin, even the most serious (*etiam ingentibus criminibus*), by gaining prevenient grace and the helps that bring sinners to the sacraments. Such efficacy is attributed to the prayer of the church which it makes in presenting the Son to the Father. Under the general category of remission of sins, no doubt the remission of venial sins and of punishment were included. The whole discussion about the difference between *ex opere operato* efficacy and the efficacy of prayer or intercession was by-passed in the text. No doubt the discussion had not clarified the question very much, and the terminology of *ex opere operato* may have been felt inopportune because of the way in which it had been taken by the reformers in their objections to the catholic mass. In any case, what is given in this proposed doctrine is just the general principle that the mass does benefit anyone for whom it is offered, and that this has to do with the remission of sins.

The fourth and final chapter was intended to resolve all the problems about practices, such as ceremonial, the use of the Roman canon, the use of latin, and private masses. It is recognized that many of these changes represent change in the practice of the church, but without deciding what dates back to apostolic times and what is of more recent vintage, the text states that change comes about through the guidance of the Holy Spirit. As for the charges against private masses, it is said that the name itself is a misnomer, for every mass celebrated by a priest, with or without the communion of a congregation, is a common sacrifice, offered by a public minister. This view was bolstered by the fact that the doctrine on order was presented at the same time as that on the mass, confirming the vision of a visible institution of priesthood and sacrifice.

### Reactions of the Conciliar Fathers[78]

The task of the *Patres* was not to speak to the heretics' opinions, as summarized in the articles, but to react to the doctrine proposed by the theologians and to suggest censures for the articles, based on what they had heard. The discussion was apparently opened mildly enough by the bishop of Trent, Cardinal Madruzzo, who proposed some minor modifications in the text on the mass and asked that the doctrine on order be placed before that on the mass, since the mass depended on the priesthood.[79] Some of the fathers of the Council did rehearse the arguments given already by the theologians, but for the most part their contribution can be read in direct relation to the doctrine presented to them. Their comments on this show what they thought about the relation of the mass to the cross and to

---

[78] Massarelli's summary of the interventions is given CT VII/1 438–459. Some written *vota* are given CT VII/2 588–689, inclusive of interventions on the sacrament of order. The list of bishops appointed to form canons and modify the doctrine is given CT VII/1 459.

[79] CT VII/1 441 25–442 3.

the supper, and what they thought about the way in which application was presented in the text.

## One or Two Sacrifices?

The distinction made between the priesthood of Aaron and the priesthood of Melchisedech drew fire. Nothing, it was insisted, should be said that could suggest the existence of two priesthoods or two sacrifices in the work of Christ and in the christian dispensation. It would be incorrect to give the impression that Christ offered one sacrifice and exercised one priesthood on the cross, leaving a different priesthood and sacrifice to the church, by reason of his action at the last supper. There are only two modes, it was said, of one sacrifice, and only one priesthood.[80] The mention of Aaron was thus eliminated from the chapter and Melchisedech alone was mentioned as figure of Christ's and the church's priesthood.

There was still some question as to how Melchisedech ought to be presented as figure. Some discussion centred on the use of Gen 14.18, or the sacrifice in bread and wine, which had been given by a number of theologians as evidence of the sacrifice of the mass. A number of bishops asked whether this text could really be used without abusing its meaning, or whether it was indeed in offering through the forms of bread and wine that Christ acted as priest according to the order of Melchisedech. Bishop Pflug, following the line of thought opened up by Tapper and Gropper, suggested that the importance of the priesthood according to Melchisedech is found in the entry of Christ into heaven, not in the offering of bread and wine. In presenting this idea, he referred to Hebrews 5.1ff., 7.25 and

---

[80] Granatensis (Granada) VII/1 445 19f.: Camerinensis (Camerino) VII/1 447 2f.: Lancianensis (Lanciano) VII/2 613 21–24: Syracusanus (Syracusa) VII/2 632 3–7. The archbishop of Cologne (Coloniensis) VII/2 676 10–16, wanted it stated that the one sacrifice, offered in two distinct ways, fulfills all the sacrificial figures of the old law.

9.12–14. These texts make no mention of Melchisedech's offering of bread and wine, but taking him as type of Christ because he is without genealogy they speak of Christ's entry into heaven through the shedding of his blood and of his eternal intercession. Pflug then proposed that it is the one offering, begun at the supper, culminating on the cross and continuing in heaven, that is represented in the eucharist. This, for him, was the real meaning of taking Melchisedech as figure of Christ's priesthood.[81]

There were two other rather ingenious suggestions about the meaning of references to Melchisedech. The bishop of Bitonto, Cornelio Musso, said that it was not only in offering under the forms of bread and wine, but by offering himself on the cross for the gentiles, that Christ acted as priest according to the order of Melchisedech, fulfilling the figure of the priest of the gentile nations.[82] The bishop of Forli, Tommaso Campeggio, seems to have been playing devil's advocate on this point. In a written *votum*, given to the secretary of the Council, he supported the use of the bread and wine comparison, but in his spoken intervention he said that Gen 14.18 could hardly be used of the eucharist. In his written opinion, if Christ were to be compared to Melchisedech it was because he was king of peace and of justice.[83]   What was brought into relief by this discussion was the question whether or not Christ had offered himself at the supper, when he instituted the mass. That he did offer himself was argued at length by Christophorus of Padua, general of the Augustinians and Council member, mostly with arguments drawn from the supper narratives.[84] A whole host of other conciliar fathers can be cited as saying that what is done in the mass is what Christ did at the supper, this implying an offering at the supper,[85] only a couple dissenting from this common view, since it would have meant that Christ anticipated the offering of the cross at the supper, with serious consequences for the theology of redemption.[86]

## Propitiation and Application

The main point questioned by the bishops in what was said about applying the mass, was that the doctrine mentioned only the baptized. The cardinal of Trent,[87] the bishops of Syracusa,[88] Constanzia[89] and Camerino,[90] as well as the Augustinian general, already mentioned,[91] all thought that non-believers should be included among the possible beneficiaries of the offering of the mass. This naturally led them to take up the distinction of modes of efficacy, since they did not want to say that the mass worked for believers and for non-believers in the same way. This meant taking up again the theological discussion, now adding to the ways for the remission of the sins and punishments of christians the way of remission for non-baptized persons. Costanzia and Syracusa, as well as Christophorus of Padua, said that the fruits could be applied or dispensed in the strict sense only for the remission of venial sin and satisfaction. For grave sinners and for non-believers, grace could be obtained by way of impetration. It has already been

---

[85] Besides the joint *votum* of Viennensis (Vienna) and Zagrabensis (Zagreb) VII/2 590 6f., Jedin, Bd. III 525, note 33, mentions Orense VII/2 450 8: Tudensis 453 11–36: Bossanensis 455 9–18: Mutinensis 455 34–456 7: Pampilonensis VII/1 456 11–21. To these can be added: Elnensis VII/1 451 31ff. Astoricensis 454 6–17: Castellimaris 457 8–19: Civitatensis Hispaniae 457 23–25. There is also a note submitted by Constantiensis VII/2 681 23–682 20.

[86] Feltrensis VII/2 612 17f.: Bituntinus VII/1 449 34–37, where however the bishop mentions a spiritual offering.

[87] CT VII/1 443 4f.

[88] CT VII/2 635 22–29.

[89] CT VII/2 640 15–17.

[90] CT VII/1 447 3.

[91] CT VII/2 662 32–663 8.

mentioned that Pflug asked for greater clarity on modes of efficacy, and that the response to the general prayers of priest and faithful should not be confused with the working of the sacrifice.

The very obscurity of this question and the diversity of views on it, led Campeggio, bishop of Forli, to warn his brothers that the Council needed to be careful in what it defined.[92] The general statement that the mass is rightly offered for the living and the dead and applied by the priest for sins, satisfactions and other necessities, seemed to be about all that could be said without entering into very muddy waters.

### Canons and Doctrine, January 1552

The bishops appointed by the papal legate, Pighio, to take account of the debate presented a set of canons on the 15th of January, and a revised version of the doctrine on the 20th of the same month.[93]

The canons adhered quite closely to the ten articles with which the theologians had begun their discussions. The material, however, was divided into thirteen canons, each with an anathema attached to it. The first five canons were explicitly doctrinal. They condemned those who deny that the sacrifice of the mass is a true and propitiatory sacrifice or that it was instituted by Christ. They also repudiated the opinions that it is a mere commemoration of the cross, or that the eucharist is sacrament and not sacrifice, or that as a mystical offering it takes away from the sufficiency of the sacrifice of the cross. This was to define the meaning of true and propitiatory as much by negation as by affirmation, for what was made clear was that any of the mentioned views were inadequate to the truth of the mass.

[92] CT VII/2 612 2ff.
[93] For the canons, cf. CT VI/1 460ff. and for the doctrine, cf. VII/1 475–483.

The other eight canons had to do with discipline or practices. They anathematized objections to the canon of the mass, to the mass's offering for the living and the dead (the main point in calling it propitiatory), to private masses, that is, masses where only the priest received communion, to the mixing of water with wine, to the silent words of consecration, to the use of latin in the mass's celebration, and to the use of ceremonial. Canon 10 condemned those who said that the mass could be celebrated in only one species, and canon 11 was a condemnation of those who wanted mass said in the vernacular, this being the way in which latin was upheld as legitimate. Needless to say, not all of these issues were necessarily thought to be beyond discussion, but the anathema affected those who were propagating ideas on them that attacked catholic practice and were connected with a denial of the mass's propitiatory character. One cannot isolate any one of these items from its immediate historical context.

It can hardly be said often enough that it is impossible to draw neat distinctions between the doctrinal content of Trent's teaching and its practical concerns. The disciplinary canons are necessary to an understanding of what the conciliar members had in mind in teaching or anathematizing doctrine, and the doctrinal concern of the time makes it clear why certain practices had in their eyes to be defended. All of the canons converge in interest on the nature of the act performed by the priest when he acted as minister of Christ.

In revising the chapters of doctrine at the end of the debate, the commission kept the division into four chapters. The principal changes made had to do with the one offering and priesthood, and with the application of fruits.

Mention of a priesthood according to Aaron was eliminated from the first chapter. In using the figure of Melchisedech to explain the New Testament priesthood, the text quoted Psalm 109.4 to say that God's oath in itself shows that the mass is a true and proper sacrifice. It is the priesthood according to the order of Melchisedech that Christ exercised in offering himself at the supper and that he continues to exercise through the ministry of the church's priests. In this way, the commission included an offering at the supper, to respond to the demand of most of the bishops, but did not take a position on how this relates to the offering of the cross or to Christ's heavenly intercession at God's right hand.

Other scriptural texts were included to confirm the teaching on the propitiatory sacrifice. These were Mal 1.10f., Dan 8.3 and 12.11, as well as 1 Cor 10.18–21. All of these had been extensively quoted by theologians and bishops alike in their arguments against reformation teachings. While the institution of the mass was located in the supper words of Jesus, no particulars in the reading of those words by Council speakers were included in the text. Instead of making it appear that this institution could be proved directly and solely from the scriptures, the text said that this is the understanding of what was done at the supper to be found in earliest tradition. Furthermore, this understanding of the mass as sacrifice and of its foundation in the supper narrative was located in the words of the canon: *Unde et memores offerimus*, etc. It was a nice twist to include the canon that the reformers reviled as one of the chief monuments of tradition to the sacrificial nature of the eucharist.

The second chapter of the revised text explained why a sacrifice beyond the cross is needed. First, the new law would be more imperfect than the law of nature and the old law if it did not have an external and visible priesthood, with corresponding sacrifice. Secondly, beyond the distribution of grace through the sacraments a means is needed to provide for what cannot be done through them. The mass, which is this sacrifice, is related to the cross because it is the continued offering of the one oblation, both priest and victim being the same, only the manner of offering being different. All fruits distributed through the mass are fruits won by the obedience of the redeemer on the cross. In this way, all suggestion or hint of a distinction between the offering of Christ and the offering of the church is removed from the doctrine.

On application of fruits, the revised text stated that among the richer fruits of the mass is the propitiatory or expiatory placation of God's anger. Placated by the mass, God in his mercy may pardon even the most grievous crimes. This mention of divine anger and its placation was actually prefaced by a long explanation using the language of divine love. It was pointed out that in the mass the faithful are reminded of the Father's love and of the love which Christ showed in his passion. This is the proper context within which to speak of expiation and satisfaction, as had been already said by some of the theologians. Avoiding another pitfall, the writers of this chapter were careful to say that grave sin is not forgiven without recourse to the sacrament of penance. What is in effect obtained through the mass for the serious sinner is the grace of repentance. Beyond this, the revision attempts no explanations further to what the original text had given. It only adds a kind of admonition to priests, saying that application is to be made according to the rules of justice and charity.

## Conclusion

The Synod suspended its work before anything further was done with this proposed doctrine and canons. Although they were not taken as the starting-point when it returned to the sacrifice of the mass in 1562, they did have an influence on further debate and on the composition of the Council's definitive teaching. Hence it is useful to summarize the positions at which the Council had arrived by the end of January, 1552.

First of all, the close connection between doctrine and practice continued to underlie the whole issue of sacrifice and propitiation. Secondly, the discussion and proposed decree centred upon the ministerial act of the priest who consecrated and offered in virtue of the priesthood. This was the node of the argument. Thirdly, it was this priestly act which was always envisaged in regard to the application of fruits. Fourthly, application of the fruits of the cross through the mass, or remission of sin and satisfaction, was what was intended by the concern over the *propitiatory* value of the sacrifice. Fifthly, on this subject there were differences of opinion among catholic scholars and bishops about the mode of efficacy which the session did not intend to adjudicate. Sixthly, the theologians and bishops could not be held guilty of the accusation that ideas about the mass's efficacy did away with the need for proper disposition and faith on the part of those who were its beneficiaries. Seventhly, the real theological issue was to explain all of this in such a way that the practice of the mass did not seem to take away from the sufficiency of the cross. Eighthly, the clearly incontrovertible point on the relation of the mass to the cross, the least intended in speaking of it as commemoration and representation, is that there is only one victim, offered on the cross and in the eucharist, and that whatever is done in benefit of sinners is done through the power of Christ. Ninthly, though the expression that Christ offers through the priest was adopted, in order to eliminate the idea that the church is an offerer distinct from Christ, no common explanation of this had been found or embraced. Though several speakers connected supper, cross, heavenly priesthood and mass, none of this was included in what was put together as doctrine.

# Chapter 4

## TRENT 1562

As mentioned, the 1562 session of the Council did not begin its discussion on the sacrifice of the mass with the canons and doctrine that had been compiled at the close of the 1551/52 session. These, however, were not ignored and their influence on the formation of the final decree voted by the Council becomes obvious when the two documents are compared. However, one must take account of how the theologians and bishops went about their work at the Council's final session.

While a number of bishops were named to prepare doctrine and canons on the sacrifice of the mass, and to draw up a list of abuses that occurred in its celebration,[1] the theologians were instructed to speak to a list of thirteen questions about doctrine and practice. This was a new format for debate, since questions were adopted instead of a listing of errors. In subject matter and concern, however, there was little difference between the questions and the earlier lists of errors.[2]

The first of the questions put to discussion asked whether the mass is only a commemoration of the sacrifice of the cross, or whether it is itself a true sacrifice. Following on this, the second question asked whether the mass can be said to take away from the sacrifice of the cross, that is, whether to hold it as a sacrifice is opposed to the sufficiency of the merits and satisfaction of the death of Christ on the cross.[3] Doctrinally, these two questions were completed by question thirteen, which asked whether the

---

[1] CT VIII 721.

[2] CT VIII 719 1–26. Jedin, Band IV/1 338, note 11, indicates that he has been unable to identify those who composed these questions.

[3] The text in both cases says *sacrificium in coena*, but this has to be a copyist's error, since the theologians' answers have to do with the *sacrificium in cruce*.

mass is a sacrifice only in the sense of being a sacrifice of praise and thanksgiving, or whether it is not indeed itself a propitiatory sacrifice. Though this precise point had not been included in the list of errors discussed at previous sessions, it had been much debated.

The third and fourth questions also had to do with matters more directly doctrinal. Thus the third had to do with the origins of the mass and asked whether this was to be found in the memorial command given by Christ at the last supper to his apostles. This, of course, meant whether the command could be understood as a command to offer Christ's body and blood, and not only a command regarding the sacrament. Following on this, the fourth question asked whether the mass was of benefit only to communicants, or whether it could be offered for the living and the dead, for sins, satisfactions and other necessities.

The questions then turned to more practical matters. The fifth was about private masses, that is, those masses at which only the priest communicates. The sixth was about the mixing of water with wine in the chalice; and the seventh concerned the proposed abrogation of the canon of the mass, because of its alleged doctrinal errors. The eighth and ninth had to do with the silent recitation of the words of consecration and the use of the vernacular in the mass, as against the use of latin. The tenth question took up the celebration of masses in honour of saints and the eleventh the use of ceremonies and vestments. The twelfth could be said to revert to doctrinal matters, since it asked whether the mystic immolation of Christ that takes place in the eucharist could be identified with the act of eating and drinking his body and blood. In other words, the question was whether sacrificial language could be simply understood as a metaphor for communion in the body and blood of Christ.

One sees that questions one to eleven followed out the order of concerns expressed in the articles of the previous session, whereas the last two took up reformation explanations of the mass that had not been included in those articles. That no doubt explains their presence at the end of the list, even though in content they relate to the first three questions.

## The Theologians

At this stage of the Council's proceedings, there was some anxiety to finish business as quickly as possible. Hence the legates presiding at the Council proposed that seventeen theologians speak to questions one to seven, and the others to the rest of the list. Each speaker was also allotted a fixed measure of time, but the first speaker, Alphonsus Salmeron, a Jesuit, broke the rule by speaking for two hours and others readily followed his example, without apparently any effort on the part of the presidency to restrain them until the debate was cut off before all had had the opportunity to speak.[4] In effect, the breaking of the rule and the division of labour meant that there was little time and little substance left for the second group of speakers. Unless they were to make meat of question thirteen on the difference between a sacrifice of thanksgiving and a sacrifice of propitiation there was little enough for them to comment upon in their set of questions, and even that was hard to do since it was ground amply covered by those who spoke to the first three questions.[5]

As far as this second group of theologians is concerned, it is enough to say that they supported the practices listed in the questions with the same arguments about their venerability that were given in previous sessions. Thus Francisco Torres could say

[4] Salmeron was paid a nice tribute by Massarelli, who in noting the length of time that he took for his intervention says that he addressed the question learnedly and reverently (*docte et pie*). One of the bishops also noted that he offended no one, which seems to have been a matter for remark: cf. CT VIII 724 24 and note 7.

[5] For the theologians' interventions cf. CT VIII 722–751. For this session, the material is available only in the record kept by the secretary of the Council, Massarelli.

that James, Mark, Clement of Rome, and Denis the Areopagite wrote the mass.[6] In this way, he included the liturgy of James, the Alexandrine liturgy of Mark, the liturgy of the Clementine letters, and through Denis the Roman liturgy, and gave them all a nice apostolic and first-century paternity. Nothing much had changed on this score since 1547.

Some of the reasons given by this second group of speakers for the silent recitation, not only of the words of consecration but of the whole canon (meaning the part from *Te igitur* onwards), and for the retention of latin in celebration are worth noting. Antonius Grossutus took the canon as a prayer that the priest says in the name of Christ, rather than something having to do with the people. It was for this reason that it was to be said silently, for in this way it could be said with reverence and attention. He compared the priest entering into the silent canon to the Lord retiring into the garden in secret.[7] Antonius de Lugo listed the words of consecration among the secret words that Christ confided to the apostles, keeping them hidden from the people.[8]

On the use of latin, there was no unanimity. Some held that in itself the vernacular could be used but that the times were not expedient to change, since in fact its use only led to abuses.[9] Others supported latin's usage as something sacred, not to be tampered with. Perhaps the most curious argument was the one which presented latin, greek and hebrew as the three sacred languages, since these were the ones to be found on the inscription over the cross of Christ.[10] The argument most contemptuous of the people was that which compared using the vernacular with casting pearls before swine.[11] All in all, these

[6] CT VIII 726 5.
[7] CT VIII 744 39–745 2.
[8] CT VIII 745 25–29.
[9] E.g. Caesar Ferrantius CT VIII 742 5–7.
[10] Franciscus de Sanctis CT VIII 743 35f.
[11] Id. 744 2f.

arguments confirm the strictly priestly approach to the mass that dominated among catholic theologians and that is basic also to the doctrinal discussions. The people's need to be instructed and served in their religious wants was certainly noted, but this did not form part of the understanding of the sacrifice of the mass as such, or of its efficacy for the church and for the remission of sin.

More attention, then, needs to be given to the formulation of doctrine, keeping in mind its relation to practice. Here it is proposed to give particular notice to what differed in this session from treatment of the issues in earlier sessions.

In arguments for the sacrificial nature of the mass, considerable attention was given to the human need for a well-structured religious system, and some indication of this found its way into the final conciliar decree. Sacrifice and priesthood were said to be rooted in natural law and to form part of the rich heritage of the old law that is taken over by the new. The fulfilment of nature and of the old law in Christ and in the church were taken to be a perfectioning of the religious system, a more perfect sacrifice and a more perfect priesthood. For the Tridentine theologians, this perfection lay in what was visible, institutional and ceremonial about the church's cult.[12] This natural and biblical analogue for mass and priesthood was no small part of the divergence between reformation practice and catholic practice, and was related to fundamental differences on

[12] Cf. Petrus de Soso CT VIII 726 20f.: 'Negare in ecclesia non esse sacrificium, est repugnare iuri naturae et divino'; Antonius Solisius 727 4–6: '. . . quod autem missa sit sacrificium probavit, quia in omni saeculo semper fuit sacrificium, ergo multo magis in ecclesia catholica et evangelica, quae est nobilior aliis'; Camillus Campegius 727 26–28: '. . . ostendit, sacrificium esse iure naturae, et propterea omnes gentes illud habere debent, cum nulla umquam gens fuerit, quae eo caruerit; ergo multo minus christiana . . .'; Ferdinandus Tricius 728 8f.; Octavianus Canus 740 20ff.; Balthasar Crispus 741 5ff.; Alphonsus Contreras 730 13ff.; Ferdinandus de Bellogiglio 729 21f.

the relation between grace and nature, or on the effects of sin on nature.

A matter which aroused some discord between the theologians was the basis of catholic belief in the mass as sacrifice. Like speakers in the previous sessions, they were following out the instructions to take arguments from the scriptures, church fathers and church authorities, but some disagreement arose as to how these arguments related to one another, and especially about the place and strength of scriptural arguments. There was a lively interlude on this score brought about by the interventions of the two Portuguese theologians sent by the king of Portugal to the Council, the one speaking on the 24th of July, and the other following him next in line, on the 26th. Franciscus Herrera scattered the scriptural arguments to the winds.[13] He refuted the proofs from the words of Christ at the supper, from 1 Cor 10.21, from Hebrews 13.10 and from Mal 1.10f., and in dismissing all appeal to the figure of Melchisedech he claimed that Christ had not offered himself at the supper to God. According to this speaker, it is not from scripture but only from tradition that the church knows that the mass is a sacrifice. That indeed is all that is necessary for belief.

The other Portuguese theologian, Didacus de Paiva, reclaimed the scriptural arguments, but not without his own way of appealing to tradition. He attempted to give a benign interpretation to the words of his fellow-countryman, saying that his real intention had been to state that tradition is needed to understand scripture, most especially the nature of the Lord's memorial command at the supper.[14] With this, Paiva would agree. Not only did he recognize the authority of the church to

[13] CT VIII 731 36–732 27.
[14] For his intervention, cf. CT VIII 732 31–734 21. On Ferrerius, he said: 'Defenditque dicta per illum monachum quia intellexit, verba illa de per se non dicere: *Sacrificate*, sed quod ita intelligenda sunt ex traditione ...' (735 5–8).

99

decree beliefs, but he deemed it necessary for church authority to have the power to establish practice. In this way, he allowed himself both to argue from scripture for the sacrifice and at the same time to entertain the hypothesis that Christ himself had not established the mass as a sacrifice, but only as a sacrament. If this hypothesis were to be granted, he said, it was within the power of the church to establish the eucharist as a sacrifice.[15]

Hubert Jedin seems to have read Paiva's words to mean that he did not hold with a self-offering of Jesus Christ at the last supper.[16] However, it would seem that he was taking the rather unique position of stating that Christ probably did offer himself, but that this was not necessary to the institution of the mass as a sacrifice, for in any case the church's power would extend to this. Most of the other theologians at this session, in holding for a self-oblation of Christ in the upper room, seem to have been influenced by the thought that this was important to the sacrificial nature of the mass, which he then instituted. Favourable arguments for this, based on the words and acts of Christ and on the offering made by Melchisedech in his prefigurement, were registered by Salmeron,[17] Antonius Solisius,[18] Camillus Campegius,[19] Ferdinandus Tricius,[20] Alphonsus Contreras,[21] and perhaps Ferdinandus de Bellogiglio.[22]

The one who developed the negative view on this point most

[15] 734 8f.: 'Si etiam Christus non instituisset eucharistiam uti sacrificium, potuisset ecclesia eam constituere, quia sacramentum et sacrificium non sunt inter se contraria . . ..'
[16] Jedin, Bd. IV/1 181f.
[17] CT VIII 724 6f.
[18] CT VIII 727 17.
[19] CT VIII 727 35–38.
[20] CT VIII 728 13.33.
[21] CT VIII 730 33.
[22] CT VIII 730 1.

fully was Franciscus Torres.[23] He dismissed the argument that Christ had offered himself on the cross according to the priesthood of Aaron, which he attributed to Salmeron, though this is not mentioned in the transcript of Salmeron's intervention. He than went on to explain the way in which Christ was a priest according to the order of Melchisedech, discounting the force of the arguments from Gen 14.18 and this text's relation to the supper. For Torres, referring to Hebrews, it was on the cross that Christ offered himself according to the order of Melchisedech; he entered fully into this priesthood by entering into heaven by the shedding of his blood, to plead for humanity at the right hand of the Father. He then related Gen 14.18 to the mass, since it is under the forms of bread and wine that the cross is commemorated and the heavenly intercession of Christ offered through the ministry of priests. Against an offering of himself at the supper, Torres brings an argument from silence. Since Paul (in Hebrews), he said, spoke so often of the shedding of blood on the cross and of the offering in the heavenly sanctuary, surely he would have mentioned an oblation at the last supper, had he known about it.[24]

[23] CT VIII 724 29–726 8, especially 725 2–22. Jedin Bd. IV/1 180 says of this intervention: 'Er gab dem Memorialcharakter der Messe ein ganz anderes Gewicht, verbunden mit dem Selbstopfer der Gläubigen', and on p. 182 mentions Torres's unwillingness to cede a self-offering by Christ at the supper. Torres indeed did give much importance to the self-offering of the faithful, but it was not this which for him constituted the memorial character of the mass. He specifically stressed that only the priest had the power to offer sacrifice, and that the spiritual offering of the faithful was to be united with this. Of Melchisedech, Torres said, 725 6–12: 'Et Paulus Heb 10.12 testatur: offerens se hostiam etc., et propterea factum esse sacerdotem in aeternum secundum ordinem Melchisedech, sedens ad dexteram Dei, exspectans donec, etc. . . . qui perpetuo interpellat pro nobis quia semel passus est in cruce.' Jedin takes no note of this part of the intervention.

[24] 725 8–10: 'Et cum Paulus 7 ad Heb meminerit saepe sacrificii cruenti in cruce, meminisset profecto aliquando de hostia incruenta in Eucharistia, si Christum in coena obtulisse credidisset.'

In this discussion about the last supper, we hear some echoes of the interventions in 1551. The question remained that of relating the mass to the cross, and deciding what part the last supper and the heavenly priesthood of Christ had in establishing the true nature of this relationship. In this session, it was the minority view which held on to the place of the heavenly priesthood in the meaning of the mass, the majority speaking more in terms of the mass as the continuation of the last supper, and finding in it some kind of anticipation of the offering on the cross. In 1551, theologians like Tapper and Gropper had seen this offering as an anticipation, perfected on the cross, continued in heaven, and represented in the mass. The issue of what Christ did at the last supper was the one that captured the major attention of the bishops, when they followed up on the interventions of the theologians in this final conciliar session.

*Doctrine and Canons, 6th August 1562*
The bishops assigned to the task presented the doctrine on the sacrifice of the mass in four chapters, and the canons or anathemas to the number of twelve, on the 6th of August.[25]

The four chapters corresponded to those composed in 1552. In the first chapter, however, the commission was clearly looking for a way around the two major points of controversy, namely, the offering of Christ at the supper and the use to be made of the figure of Melchisedech. The text did not say that Christ offered himself at the last supper under the species of bread and wine, nor did it deny this. When at the last supper, it reads, the Lord changed bread and wine into his body and blood, he gave himself to his apostles to be eaten and offered, saying: Do this in commemoration of me. By these words, the text continues, the church has always understood that a command was given to the apostles, and through them to all

[25] CT VIII 751–754 24; 754 25–755 6.

priests, to offer sacrifice in Christ's memory. That was to relate the offering of the mass to the words of Christ, without deciding the point about his own self-offering. On Melchisedech, the text said that an added reason for instituting the sacrifice in bread and wine was to show that by the Father's oath Christ was confirmed as priest according to the order of Melchisedech. This was also a way of leaving open to discussion whether Christ exercised this priesthood in the supper or not, or whether the institution simply prefigured the heavenly priesthood, which according to the minority opinion was the true exercise of the order of Melchisedech.

The scriptural texts cited as confirmation of the church's understanding of the Lord's words are 1 Cor 10.16f. and Mal 1.10f. Citing the scripture narrative as found in the Roman canon, the text stated that in blessing, consecrating, offering and ordering priests to offer, Christ instituted the essentials of the rite of the mass. It is noticeable that no mention was made of communion. Finally, this first chapter added a theological elaboration on the meaning of sacrifice, saying that it is a giving back to God of gifts originally received from him.

The second chapter explained the need to have a sacrifice and its relation to the cross. The mass was described as a memorial sacrifice, different from the cross only in the way of offering, offerer and offered being the same in both sacrifices. Three reasons were given why the church needs this memorial sacrifice. First, it is required for the application of the fruits of the cross. Second, it is more universal than the sacraments, which benefit only those who receive them. Third, an external and visible sacrifice belongs to the perfection of the law of the gospel.

The third chapter, on application of fruits, was almost identical with the corresponding chapter of 1552, with the exception of one rather significant point. The argument that the mass placates the anger of God was dropped, and a more nuanced statement substituted for it. This said that the one who is immolated in this sacrifice is propitiation and propitiatory offering (*propitiatio et propitiatorium*), an expression which still relates to the imagery of satisfaction but does not mention divine anger. The text still kept the grace given to even hardened sinners for their repentance to the fore, rather than the satisfaction for punishment and venial sin.

The fourth chapter had a word to say for all the practices abhorred by the reformers, and in this it stuck to the point and purpose of the corresponding chapter in 1552, but the reasons given for them were somewhat changed. Ceremonies and rites were described as the visible signs of religion, that remind us of invisible mysteries. The canon of the mass was said to be sound in doctrine, when interpreted according to the meaning of the orthodox fathers of the church, the insinuation no doubt being that this the reformers neglected to do. The whole canon is best said *submissa voce*, because of the mystery which it enacts. The retention of latin was upheld because it was thought to serve reverence for the mystery and the unity of the church, which thus prayed everywhere in the one tongue and used the same formulas. The composers of the text were not prepared to see any inconvenience in this for the faithful who did not understand latin, for they added that at least on Sundays and on feast-days the faithful could and should be instructed in the knowledge of the mysteries and of the faith. The text repeated the claim of the previous session that there is no such thing as a private mass, because the priest always acts, even in private, as a public minister in celebrating the mass. Christ himself probably put water in the chalice at the last supper, and in any case this sign recalls the water flowing from the side of Christ on the cross and the union of the people with Christ in the mass. These were in fact the three reasons most often offered by the speakers at the Council in favour of this practice.

There were twelve canons, taking up the points asked in the

thirteen questions put to the theologians at the beginning of the session. One canon joined together two questions, namely on the offering of the mass *pro aliis* and on the difference between communion and sacrifice. There was also a change in order, question thirteen transformed into an anathema on those who held only for a sacrifice of thanksgiving being given second place. This meant that the condemnation of those who held that the mass was only a commemoration of the cross and not a sacrifice was followed by a curse on those who held that it was only a sacrifice of thanksgiving, not one of propitiation. This was a logical sequence and followed out the order of the debate as pursued in all three sessions on the mass.

## Interventions of Conciliar Fathers[26]

The bishops had some complaints about the form in which the decree was proposed, and some about the substance or content. The first complaint about the form had to do with the proposed decree's prolixity. Many thought that the chapters could be shorter and should touch only on the points of controversy in which catholics were engaged with evangelical protestants. Some even suggested that the canons alone would be sufficient. The second complaint about the form had to do with a lack of coordination between the chapters and the canons, since the two sections of the decree did not take the points of doctrine and practice in the same order.

As for substance or content, that which captured the practically exclusive attention of the bishops was the omission of a direct mention of any self-offering of himself by Christ in the supper room.[27] From the 11th to the 18th of August, the sessions

[26] CT VIII 755–790.

[27] A somewhat dated but interesting discussion of this debate is found in E. Jamouelle, 'L'unité sacrificielle de la Cène, la Croix et l'Autel au Concile de Trente', *Ephemerides Theologicae Lovaniensis* XXII (1946) 34–69, and 'Le sacrifice eucharistique au Concile de Trente', *Nouvelle Revue Théologique* 67

appear to have turned largely into a matter of each bishop in turn declaring himself either for or against such a mention in the first chapter of the proposed document. Those who wanted this included were: the cardinal archbishop of Trent, the patriarchs of Jerusalem and Venice, and the archbishops or bishops of Otranto, Naxos, Florence, Rossano, Ragusa, Zara, Matera, Sorrento, Ianua, Palermo, Cava, Mylopotamos, Caiazzo, Città Castellana, Philadelphia (Asia Minor), Caorle, Castro, Chioggia, S. Agata dei Goti, Ajaccio, Segovia, Rimini, Capo d'Istria, Littere, Reggio Emilia, Coimbra and Terni. Those who pronounced themselves unfavourable to such mention, either because they thought that Christ did not then offer himself or because they found that it could not be proved from the scriptures, or because they thought it a matter of legitimate dispute, were Guerrero, archbishop of Grenada, and the bishops of Braga, Bertinoro and Brugnato.[28]

By the 18th of August, there had apparently been time to give the matter some thought, since that day the arguments began to show more complexity and theological sophistication, marked by an awareness that this was not purely a matter of 'sic vel non'. Euctace du Bellay, archbishop of Paris, argued at first along well-worn tracks, saying that if Christ had not offered himself at the supper the mass could not be a sacrifice, and wanting to use Gen 14.18 in this sense. He then went on, however, to try to give some explanation of this offering in such a way that it would not have a negative effect on the theology of the once-for-all offering of the cross. The core problem in this discussion was that since all Christ's acts were considered to be of infinite value, the offering at the supper would seem to render the cross unnecessary. Du Bellay countered this difficulty by saying that

(1945) 1121–1139. More recently, cf. H. Holstein, 'La Cène et la Messe dans la doctrine du sacrifice eucharistique de Concile de Trente', in *Humanisme et Foi Chrétienne* (Paris: Beaochesne 1976) 649–662.

[28] All of these interventions are to be found in CT VIII 755–765.

at the supper Christ began to suffer, and since this suffering was continuous with the suffering of the passion it was already expiatory, but expiatory by way of moral unity with the cross.[29] This intervention, whether its reasoning proved acceptable or not, helped to clarify what theological problem was at stake. First, the question was not simply whether or not Christ offered himself to the Father at the supper, but whether if it occurred it was expiatory or propitiatory. Secondly, if expiatory, what relation did it have to the offering on the cross.

Subsequent speakers took the term *expiatory* as their cue. Duimius de Gliricis, bishop of Veglia, argued the counterposition. He put forward the idea that like all Christ's acts during his life-time the supper could be said to have been a self-offering, in as much as it was an act of obedience and reverence to God, but that only the cross was expiatory, since only through the cross was reconciliation effected between humanity and God. The figure of Melchisedech's offering could even be used of the supper, because this was only a sacrifice of thanksgiving and not one of expiation, and there was no problem in admitting that Christ offered a sacrifice of thanksgiving the night before he died. The bishop of Veglia did not hold much truck with the argument that in the mass the church repeats what Christ did at the supper, since for him this was clearly not the case: at the supper Christ was mortal and subject to suffering, as offered in the mass he is glorious and free from suffering (*impassibilis*).[30]

On the 19th of August, the bishop of Modena spoke in much the same way as Veglia, distinguishing between the eucharistic sacrifice of the supper and the expiatory sacrifice of the cross.[31]

[29] CT VIII 765 33–766 10, especially 765 39f.: 'Nam in coenae oblatione coeperat pati, et fuit contimiata cum illa crucis, fuitque expiatoria, quia est eadem cum illa crucis.'
[30] CT VIII 766 18–767 13.
[31] CT VIII 767 27–768 21.

The same day, the bishop of Leiria, Caspar de Casala, began a long intervention, which he completed only at the following general assembly.[32] He gave five arguments in favour of a propitiatory offering at the supper. First of all, he claimed that this had been the constant teaching of the *doctores ecclesiae*. Then he quoted Thomas Aquinas (S. Th. 1ae 2ae, q. 102, art. 3) to the effect that if any offering of himself by Christ at the supper is admitted, this had to be a propitiatory one. In other words, he could not agree with Veglia's and Modena's proposition that Christ had offered a eucharistic but not a propitiatory sacrifice. Leiria found that the supper met the definition of a true sacrifice in the text of Thomas, which says that whenever something is killed, poured out or eaten, this is a true sacrifice. Thirdly, he found that the supper fulfilled *all* the sacrifices of the Old Testament, which of course include expiatory ones. Fourthly, he argued from the propitiatory character of the mass to the propitiatory character of the act of Christ at the supper, since at the mass the priest repeats what Christ did then. Fifthly, since the supper represented the cross which it anticipated, it had to be of the same kind as that which it represented.

Having to his own satisfaction proved his point, Leiria went on to explain the meaning of Hebrews 10.12 and 14, which speaks of only one oblation whereby Christ expiated for sin. His major point was that on the cross and at the supper that which was offered was identical.[33] Following up on this point, he invoked Thomas Aquinas once more (S. Th. 3, q. 83, art. 5, ad 3m) to connect the acts of Christ at the supper with what he did on the cross. The Blessed Thomas, he said, showed that Christ perfected his passion in several stages, of which the supper was the third and the cross the fourth. Between these stages there is a

[32] CT VIII 768 43–770 17.

[33] CT VIII 769 31f.: 'Una igitur et eadem hostia coena et illa crucis; una itaque oblatione, id est una hostia.' Does this mean one victim and one offering, or does it twice repeat that there is one victim?

unity of intention and purpose.[34] A third argument which for Leiria reconciled cross and supper was that according to the same Blessed Thomas (S. Th. 3, q. 48, art. 1, ad 2m) Christ merited and satisfied for sin by all the deeds of his life, but this did not render the cross superfluous because in God's plan it was required that Christ lay down his life. In the life of Christ, as when he cured the paralytic and forgave Magdalen, the bishop found not only merit but also anticipation of the merits of the cross by way of their application. If Christ could on such occasions anticipate the cross, there was no problem in seeing him do so at the supper when he offered himself for the apostles. It is in this last point that one sees what exactly was often intended in the discussion when it was asked whether the supper was propitiatory. The distinction between the particularity of beneficiaries in the mass and the communality of beneficiaries of the cross, embracing the whole world, was applied to the supper, where Christ was deemed to offer himself not for all sinners but for the apostles, who supped with him.

As transcribed by Massarelli, the bishop's intervention is not a master-piece of logic or clear exposition, though it may have sounded clearer in the council chamber. In any case, Leiria seems to have combined three lines of thought in speaking to the propitiatory or expiatory character of Christ's self-offering at the last supper. First of all, the supper and the cross are to be seen

---

[34] Leiria was here quoting St. Thomas's allegorical explanation of the actions of the priest at the mass, from the beginning to the pax, where he divides the passion into nine stages to correspond to nine parts of the mass. The stages of the passion, he says, begin with the betrayal and end with the resurrection. The second stage is the selling of Christ for thirty pieces of silver, the third the anticipation of the passion at the supper, the fourth the actual passion, the fifth the shedding of blood and the stretching of the limbs on the cross, the sixth the prayers of Christ on the cross, the seventh the three hours he hung there, and the eighth the separation of body and soul. Leiria only takes up the supper and the passion, no doubt compressing stages four to eight into one for the sake of argument.

as one act, because the victim offered in both cases is the same, and the offerer is the same. Secondly, there is merit and satisfaction in all Christ's deeds, reaching a high-point in the unity of the passion and the supper. Thirdly, since all Christ's merits and satisfactions were one in order and intention with the cross, he could and did anticipate the fruits of the cross in what he did for others. If he could and did forgive sins and heal the sick during his lifetime, having already acquired merit that had its value both from the nature of his person and from the anticipation of his passion, then there is no problem about his offering of himself for his apostles at the supper, when he had already entered more immediately into the way of his passion.

Though the bishop of Adria was honest enough to admit himself ignorant of the theology of Thomas Aquinas,[35] many of the bishops whose interventions followed that of the bishop of Leiria seem to have been impressed by his arguments and erudition. His ideas enabled them both to advocate a true offering at the supper and to maintain the unique character of the cross.

Some, however, had their own particular explanations and theories to offer. The bishop of Senigallia, de Ruvere, accepted the expiatory self-offering of Christ at the supper, but qualified it as inchoative or habitual, rather than actual.[36] He obviously wanted to differentiate between the formal intention of Christ at the supper and the efficacy of the cross. He implied that though Christ could have the same mind of giving himself up for sinners in the supper and on the cross, the two acts could not have the same formal meaning and efficacy, since only the cross was truly (*proprie*) expiatory. To say in this context that the offering of Christ at the supper was inchoatively expiatory really amounted to nothing more than saying that there was

[35] CT VIII 711 23–25.
[36] CT VIII 772 11–32.

continuity of thought and action during the whole of Christ's life, and especially between what he did at the supper and what he did on the cross, but that redemption was won on the cross.

The bishops of Almeria and Luca tried to resolve the supposed dilemma in another way.[37] They distinguished two kinds of sacrifice, one of expiation and another of reconciliation. The first kind actually makes satisfaction for sin, the second actually reconciles humanity with God. This was to use the notion of redemption which required that proper satisfaction has to be made to God for sin, and that without it there is no reconciliation, but that beyond reconciliation there is also satisfaction to be made. According to these two speakers, the cross of Christ was a sacrifice of both satisfaction or expiation and reconciliation, while the supper was one of expiation but not reconciliation, since God's plan made reconciliation dependent on the death of Christ on the cross. A self-offering of himself at the supper by Christ would, however, certainly be a worthy act and so would pay honour and satisfaction for offence to God. As for what ought to be included in the Council's teaching, Almeria suggested that it would be enough to say in a general way that Christ offered himself at the supper, without going into the specifics of expiation and reconciliation, since such matters were disputed among the fathers of the Council and did not belong to the necessary doctrine of the faith.

Still on the issue of Christ's self-offering at the supper, Didace de Léon, titular bishop of a see in parts unknown, argued, as the Acts say, *in parte negativa*.[38] In effect, his position turned out to be not very different from the alleged opposite view of Leiria. Didace proposed that the sacrifice which took place at the supper could be seen as a peace-offering, or sacrifice of

---

[37] Almeria CT VIII 777 35–778 19; Luca CT VIII 783 36–784 3.

[38] CT VIII 782 26–783 2. The title given to him is Columbriensis or Columbricensis, but it is not known where this is, or what titular see it is.

thanksgiving, as the theologians had named the peace-offerings of the Old Testament, but not as a sacrifice of propitiation. By way of refuting a biblical argument, he said that it was wrong to base one's opinion on the present tense of verbs in the supper narrative: the Council had given its approval to the Vulgate, and in the Vulgate the word reads *tradetur*, not *traditur*. As for *datur*, he interpreted this word to mean *incipit dari*. Hence, for Didace, the authentic version of the supper narrative refers not to something taking place in the present of the occasion, but to something to take place in the future, to wit the crucifixion. The term *incipit dari* was the speaker's way of expressing his own view, since he expressed by it a continuity from supper to cross. In other words, for him the offering consummated on the cross had begun in the supper.[39] In effect, this statement of the matter is really equivalent to the opinion that if it is taken as one with the cross, then the supper offering can be called expiatory. As a practical proposal, Didace of parts unknown agreed with the bishop of Almeria that the Council should be content not to qualify the self-offering of Christ at the supper but to give it simple mention.

The bishop of Alife began his intervention by following out Leiria's opinions, repeating that though expiatory the merits and satisfactions of Christ that preceded the crucifixion could not be meted out if Christ had not died. He also took the view that the will of Christ at the supper was the same as his will on the cross, and so had its own anticipatory efficacy.[40] At this

---

[39] Cf. i.c. 782 36: 'Et licet sit eadem hostia coenae et crucis, oblatio tamen una est, scilicet crucis, quae initiata est in coena, sed in cruce consummata; una tamen est oblatio, illa crucis.'

[40] CT VIII 784 4–40. Cf. 31–34: '. . . illud Christi sacrificium (in coena) non habuit efficaciam a cruce, sed a seipso, cum Christus de per se efficax sit, sicut et sacramentum in missa ex se efficaciam habet, quia et obi Christus; sed nisi oblatio crucis facta fuisset, non potuisset nobis applicari.' The intention seems to be that all Christ's acts have merit and satisfaction enough for sinners, but it is only because we have been reconciled through the cross that these are

point, the bishop took the argument a step further by drawing together not only supper and cross, but supper, cross, heavenly intercession and mass, in a way reminiscent of the interventions at the earlier session of the Council of Tapper and Gropper.

Iacobus Lainez (or Diego Lainez), general of the Jesuits, who had been present at the previous session as a theologian of the pope, and whose admission to the Council as a full member was a historic occasion, since as a Jesuit he was considered to be of the secular and not of the regular clergy, was the last to speak to the canons and chapters of the proposed decree.[41] He wanted to allow that the supper was a propitiatory offering, but held to the distinction between the universality of the cross's beneficiaries and the particularity of the application of supper and mass. It was for the apostles and not for all humanity, he pointed out citing John's gospel, that Christ prayed at the supper, just as it is for the baptized and not for all humanity that the priest prays and applies the mass. The cross is applied to non-christians through the sacraments, and this allows them to benefit from the mass, which is offered for post-baptismal sins and graces.

It was on the basis of this distinction, allowing for a restricted application of the supper, in virtue of the cross, that Lainez proposed a number of arguments in favour of the expiatory nature of the supper. The first one was that Christ needed to fulfill what was prefigured in Melchisedech by offering under the forms of bread and wine. Then he argued that since the consecration is a mystical action, whereby something is done to the thing offered, it verifies the definition of sacrifice, and that since Christ consecrated at the supper he must have sacrificed at the supper. A third argument of the Jesuit general was that the passion began at the supper; and a fourth that if Christ offered

applied. The same holds for the benefits given to the apostles at the supper, and through the supper, where of course the reconciliation of the cross had to be anticipated.

[41] CT VIII 786 39–788 4.

thanks this itself had to be expiatory, because such was the quality of Christ's thanksgiving that it too had to be expiatory. The fifth argument was not much different, since it concluded to the expiatory value of all Christ's acts from the fact that they were all done out of infinite love. Summing up, Lainez concluded that the passion comprehended, and presumably by this he meant consummated, all Christ's acts, since the same infinite charity that inspired his passion and death inspired all his earthly deeds.[42] In one sense, one could say that Lainez had proved too much, since at this juncture the supper was hardly a distinct case but just one of a series of actions in the life of Christ, all of which anticipated the passion and all of which were done out of the same love as the giving up of himself in death.

Thus the discussion ended with much the same kind of confused statement that had marked its entire course. The Fathers of the Council found themselves in something of a dilemma. They recognized that the one unique sacrifice of redemption was the cross and death of Jesus Christ, and they also recognized that the reality of the mass lay in its representative character and that all its value came from the cross. At the same time, they were much moved by the desire to play up its sacrificial character, since this was fundamental to the needs of application of the fruits of the cross, as they saw the christian dispensation, and they also seem to have been convinced that true religion needed true sacrifice as part of its cult. It is important to note that for them expiatory or propitiatory continued to mean making satisfaction, and the ability to distinguish between reconciliation with God and the making of

---

[42] CT VIII 787 28–30: 'Et si erat initium passionis, ergo expiavit; et si erat sanguis Christi, ergo expiavit; et si erat gratiarum actionis, ergo expiavit, quia gratiarum actio Christi est expiatoria', and CT VIII 787 39f.: '. . . passio Christi comprehendit omnes actus Christi, qui ea omnia eadem caritate fecit, quae tamen in cruce magis cognoscitur.' Not only is there logic in these statements, but also a nice touch of rhetoric.

satisfaction, and thus between the grace of communion with God and various species of remission, allowed them to find expiation already made at the supper, even though reconciliation came only with the cross. At the same time, it is interesting to see that the very need to debate the quality of the supper was the occasion to broaden reflection upon the mystery of redemption celebrated in the eucharist so as to include all the deeds of Christ's flesh, as well as his heavenly priesthood and intercession. It was the fact that they disposed only of the categories of sacrifice, and of merit and satisfaction, wherein to pursue this reflection that makes it look very scholastic and even confused to us today, when we compare it, for example, with the paragraph in the Lima statement which says:

> Christ himself with all that he has accomplished for us and for all creation (in his incarnation, servanthood, ministry, teaching, suffering, sacrifice, resurrection, ascension and sending of the Spirit) is present in this *anamnesis*, granting us communion with himself. The eucharist is also the foretaste of his *parousia* and of the final kingdom.[43]

The real Babylonian Captivity of the eucharist at the time of Trent was not the desire for filthy lucre, whatever abuses were practised in its administration, but the fixation of categories and the wedding of these categories to a cultic system, which would have been gravely disrupted were priests to cease offering and applying masses for the living and the dead. The debate in its various attempts to work out the relation of supper, cross, heavenly intercession and mass, within these categories, showed such confusion and difference of opinion that we are not surprised that the final decision was to follow the advice of those who thought it better to mention Christ's offering at the supper without qualifying it, and to go lightly on the explanations of

---

[43] *Baptism, Eucharist and Ministry*, p. 11, no. 6.

how the mass benefits the living and the dead, content with the clear affirmation that it does.

## Doctrine and Canons, 5th September 1562[44]

The doctrine and canons were revised in light of the discussion at the plenary assemblies. Since what was proposed on the 5th of September differs little from what was eventually decreed and promulgated, the text can be explained noting the few changes that were introduced before the final voting at the end of the session.

The preamble to the doctrine states the method followed. Teaching is drawn from the scriptures, tradition and church authority. These are to be taken as authorities that converge, rather than as distinct arguments, each complete in itself. In this way, the Council got over the difficulty about proofs from scripture, since in what is taken from it, it is not a line of exact exegesis that is proposed but the understanding of it that has always been found in the church. The content of the chapters in this final document of the synod is less prolix than the text proposed at the beginning of the 1562 session, in keeping with the observations made by the fathers. For clarity's sake, the material is divided into eight, instead of four, chapters. A ninth chapter provides the preamble to the canons, so that the connection between the two parts of the decree may be made. An attempt was clearly made by the commission in composing this decree to eliminate whatever did not pertain to the controversies surrounding the mass and to whatever the Council felt needed to be defended against the reformers. The points therefore that were given special consideration were the propitiatory nature of the sacrifice of the mass, its application for the living and the dead, the relation to the cross, and whatever practices were attacked because of their connection

---

[44] CT VIII 909–912; DS 1738–1759.

with catholic thought on the mass's efficacy and nature.

Since the text now under consideration is the one decreed by the Council, and belongs to catholic dogma and teaching, it can be spoken of in the present tense, putting into the past only those few points that were changed between the 5th of September and the end of the session. The first chapter opens with the statement that redemption is solely through the sacrifice of the cross, thus making sure that there can be no discussion of the mass outside this context. In instituting the mass at the last supper, Christ is said to have offered himself to the Father under the species of bread and wine, but it is neither affirmed nor denied that this offering was expiatory. Clearly, the debate among the fathers was kept in mind and the question left open to a variety of interpretations. Whatever can be said about the majority opinion, it was not made part of the church's magisterial teaching.

Though no qualification is attached to Christ's offering at the supper, it is connected with the priesthood according to the order of Melchisedech, the institution of the mass as a visible sacrifice, and the ordination of the apostles as priests, with power to celebrate and offer the sacrifice. The purpose is to show that the mass originated at the last supper and that it belongs to the essential order of the church as it springs from Christ. The figure of Melchisedech is mentioned, since this had had such a prominent place in catholic apologetics and in the debates of all the conciliar sessions. A certain amount of circumlocution, however, is employed, which echoes some of the arguments proposed against the use of the figure, or some of the doubts about the right way of introducing it. The test on the 5th of September had said that Christ offered himself in bread and wine, in order to show (*ut ostenderet*) that he is a priest according to the order of Melchisedech. In light of the questions raised in the debate, it is probable that the commission chose not to say that he exercised this priesthood at the supper, but that the offering in bread and wine showed that he is such a priest. This left it open either to posit an exercise of this priesthood in the offering at the supper, or to see in Christ's act at the supper an anticipatory manifestation of the priesthood whereby in the shedding of his blood he entered into the heavenly sanctuary. The approved version of the text has substituted *declarans* for *ut ostenderet*, but this seems to be stylistic rather than substantive. The gerund may have been seen as a better way than the purposive clause to qualify the act of Christ as one in which he showed forth the nature of his priesthood. In any case, the text intends to connect the priesthood according to the order of Melchisedech with the mass, for its mention is collated with the institution of the mass and its priesthood. One could connect the mass with this priesthood in any of the ways proposed by the bishops and the theologians during the debate, but the Council wanted to associate itself with the patristic tradition that linked the priesthood of Christ according to the order of Melchisedech with the mass, in at least a general way.

It is not only in the teaching about the figure of Melchisedech that one finds echoes of the conciliar debate and the nuances that go with them. These echoes are found also in the stress on visible sacrifice and its need, granted that the mention of a visible religious system is muted in comparison with the earlier text. Similarly, in mention of the constitution of the apostles as priests at the supper, one sees the desire to assure that the efficacy of the priest's act in offering and applying the mass is attributed to the power of Christ. In what is said, however, about the priesthood of the apostles and its origins, it is very important to be aware of the council's methods in presenting arguments and interpretations, lest we take to be taught things that are not. As mentioned in the preamble to the document, the Council's decree does not propose exegesis of the scriptures, nor historical interpretations. Its point in attributing the institution of the priesthood to the act of Christ at the supper is drawn from what it proposes as the church's constant way of finding its faith in the scriptural text. There is no claim made to a historical reconstruction, by way of fixing the exact moment at which the priesthood was instituted, for on order and ministry the Tridentine fathers had at least a glimmer of what was perfectly clear at the time of the Second Vatican Council, namely, that the early history of ministry and order is obscure. The language of institution as used at Trent is meant to emphasize that the church's organisms, sacraments and sacrifice have their power and efficacy from Christ. The church, it was taught, had always believed this, and it had traditionally expressed this belief in a particular reading of the scripture texts, especially the texts of the supper narrative. The ecclesial reading of these texts is corroborated in the second half of the chapter by reference to other scriptural figures and passages.

Considerable prominence is given to the image of a new Pasch and to the idea that the mass is the memorial of Christ's passage to the Father, through the shedding of his blood. Reference is also made to Mal 1.11, to 1 Cor 10.21 and to all the sacrifices of the old law, each in its own way prefiguring the sacrifice of Christ and its representation in the mass. Though these references are given in a somewhat polemical and apologetic way, in order to enhance belief in the sacrificial nature of the mass, their retention carries a potential richness for eucharistic teaching.

The second chapter deals in a rather subdued and careful way with the relation of the mass to the cross and of its application for the living and the dead, according to tradition and custom. It starts by connecting the doctrine of the sacrifice with the doctrine of the real presence, saying that the same Christ who offered himself on the altar of the cross is contained and immolated in an unbloody manner in the mass. Further on in the chapter, this is qualified by the statement that the victim is the same and that Christ now offers himself through the ministry of priests, who offered himself then on the cross, only the manner of offering being different. Here we see how the decree reflects the one common and certain point of all the conciliar debates, namely, the identity of the victim, and then deals with the more difficult point of the relation of the priest offering to Christ. The statement is actually open to several interpretations of this relation, or of the sense in which Christ now offers himself through the priest. It is the identity of the principal offerer, Christ, that is pressed, not the identity of the act of offering. One could say that the original act of offering is represented in the mass in a sacramental way, this being the difference in the mode of offering, but one could also say that a new act of offering is posited, and still retain the Council's teaching. The opinion expressed at Bologna in 1547 by several theologians that the present offering of Christ consists in the fact that he has given the church the power to make its own distinct offering of his body and blood, and that he is the instrument of the satisfactions and graces obtained through this offering, is certainly not favoured by the Council's way of speaking, but neither is it clearly and unambiguously eliminated as a possible meaning. The different interventions that connected the mass with the cross through Christ's heavenly intercession, or through the oblation made at the supper, could also be reconciled with what is decreed. In other words, one sees the whole sequence of the debate reflected in the finesse of the final statement, which leaves the way open to theologians to retain their various explanations as part of their arsenal, provided it is clearly held that the sacrifice of the mass is totally dependent on the cross and that its efficacy for sinners is totally from the power and merit of Christ.

In making this connection between mass and cross, the Council intends to explain the teaching on the propitiatory nature of the sacrifice. That was the point of controversy, and so that is the major point of magisterial teaching. Once again, all the problems of the debate find echo in the choice of statement and in the attempt to clarify major issues without foreclosing theological discussion on modalities. To begin with, it is made clear that the propitiatory fruit of the mass is accessible only to those who approach God with faith and reverence, and truly contrite for their sins. In this, the Council answers the major objections of the reformers that regard the precise meaning of *ex opere operato* efficacy, while completely avoiding that term. Secondly, it once again gives primacy among the effects of the mass to the grace of repentance that is given to sinners through God's mercy,[45] rather than to the application of satisfactions and merits for the just. These, however, are included in the general statement that the mass can be rightly offered for the living and the dead, for sins, punishment, satisfactions and other necessities. At this point, the Council retains a rather standard language and makes no attempt to sort out the mode of application, whether, that is, it is by way of *ex opere operato* efficacy or by way of suffrage and intercession. While noting the conciliar abstinence on points of controversy, one may also suggest that the root of the problem, left unresolved by the Council, is how to reconcile the appeal to divine mercy through intercession in remembrance of Christ, which the Conciliar text places in the forefront, with the computations of merits, punishments and satisfactions inherited from the medieval penitential system as categories of explanation. It is of considerable note that the language of application has been dropped from the decreed teaching of the Council, but not the language of satisfaction. The Council seems to favour the mode of intercession or suffrage over the mode of application, analogous to

---

[45] The word is *dimittit*, not *remittit*. The operations of loosing, which is the way to translate *dimittit*, are liable to be more varied than those suggested by remission. A slight revision in the text before voting made it clear that grave sins were not directly forgiven through the mass, but that what it obtains for serious sinners is the grace of repentance.

administrative justice, by placing the loosing of grave sins through God's mercy to the fore, but it has not freed itself entirely from the language of medieval theology.

It has been noted from the debates that the theologians and bishops at Trent always had the act of the priest in mind when they discussed the propitiatory nature of the mass. There is no reason to believe that this was not still the case at the end of the Council, particularly because at a later point in the decree it is said that the act of the priest is always a public act and that this justifies the given modes of celebration, but it is interesting that a specific mention of application of the fruits of the mass by the priest is dropped from the definitive text. In other words, as a result of conciliar discussion and internal controversy the synod had learned to be circumspect in those statements which purport to give magisterial teaching, leaving room and indeed need for further theological clarification, as well as for differences of opinion.

In order to avoid giving the impression of offering a complete teaching on the eucharist, rather than simply a resolution of essential conflict, this chapter was considerably shortened. All preliminaries about remembering the love of God and the love of Christ in the mass are eliminated. Likewise, no mention is made of glory among the ends of the mass, no doubt because it was felt unnecessary to enter into the debate as to whether glory is merited by the just or given to them as gratuity. On the one hand, such omissions were opportune and made the conciliar purposes much clearer. Historically, however, they may have had pejorative effects on catholic belief and piety. Despite the intention of the Conciliar fathers, from the Catechism of the Council of Trent onwards catholics tended to take the Tridentine teaching on the eucharist as a full and adequate statement of catholic belief and practice. In this sense, the conciliar abstinence may have backfired down the centuries.

Within the context of the Council itself, one sees that the

meaning of the doctrine, and still more of the corresponding canon, on the propitiatory character of the sacrifice of the mass is quite jejune. It is more than a sacrifice of praise and thanksgiving if this is understood as having nothing to do with the remission of sins through the mass; it is not only the communion in the body and blood of those sharing in its celebration, but it can be offered for the absent, living and dead, benefiting them for the remission of their sins. What is the precise nature of this benefit, and how it comes about through the operation of the mass, is not included in the magisterial use of the word *propitiatory*. The general statement 'for sins, punishments, satisfactions and other necessities' was apparently taken as a standard and traditional one, and is not to be pressed too hard for specific determinations of meaning. The relation of this doctrinal teaching to practices of offering for the living and the dead has certainly to be appreciated, for it is this system which is thereby declared meaningful in relation to the eucharistic heritage of the church, but in the end the doctrine is stated in sufficiently general terms not to make some changes in the cultic system incompatible with it.

The other six chapters of the decree dealt with the practical matters that explicated all that was bound up with this teaching. Chapter three treats of masses offered in honour of saints, and chapter four of the venerability, orthodoxy and piety of the Roman canon. Chapter five defends all manner of ceremonial, saying that it constitutes those visible signs that induce the faithful to religion, piety and contemplation. Apparently such non-verbal inducements were deemed preferable to whatever the people might pick up by hearing the scriptures and the oral prayers of the eucharist in their own language.

On masses in which only the priest communicates, the Council in chapter six approves and commends this practice, while at the same time it goes beyond the proposals of previous schemata by recommending more frequent communion to the faithful. It is said that the Council would like to see (*optaret*) some faithful communicate in all masses, so that they would obtain greater fruits from the sacrifice. In the final text, *aliqui fideles* becomes *fideles adstantes*, so that the recommendation touches all those who are present at a mass, a recommendation which remained a dead letter until very recently. This position was certainly very different to some of the cautions about frequent communion heard in conciliar interventions. At the same time, one notices how the language separates the participation of the faithful in the eucharist from the participation of the priest. They continue to be designated as those who assist at mass, the word *adstantes* being so very different from the traditional liturgical language of *circumstantes*. It is also the priest who is said to offer the sacrifice, whereas the people benefit from its fruits.

It is also in this context of so-called private masses that the role of the priest is further specified. It is affirmed that whatever the circumstances of his offering, he always acts as public minister of the church, and the faithful communicate spiritually in every mass which the priest sacramentally celebrates. Here a distinction is made between *sacerdos sacramentaliter communicat* and *populus spiritualiter communicet* which in the context is quite innocuous but which was liable to be used in support of a particularly hierarchical eucharistic theology. In the context, what is being explained is the mass at which the priest alone receives communion, and it is said that though this is the case the people always share spiritually in the offering which he makes as public minister. The terms, however, can be unfortunately applied to mean a difference between the sacramental act of offering, which pertains to the priest, and spiritual communion in this act, which pertains to the people.[46] In any case, the

---

[46] This is the usage made of the distinction by Pope John Paul II, which is discussed in the first chapter.

Council legitimizes the various usages of private mass, by reason of a theology of the sacramental role of the priest which separates it from community celebration, and this simply allowed the medieval system of worship to continue uninhibited.

Chapter seven of the decree states that it is right to mix water with wine, since Christ is believed to have done so at the supper,[47] and because it has the twofold symbolism already noted in previously proposed schemata. Chapter eight is notably mild on the conflict between proposals for the use of the vernacular and proposals to retain latin. While the synod admits that there is much in the mass which if understood adds to the people's instruction, it does not deem it expedient to adopt the use of the vernacular. Given this decision, pastors and others with the care of souls are exhorted to instruct the faithful on the meaning of the scriptures and on the meaning of the mass and its ceremonies, at least on Sundays and feast-days.

The twelve original canons were now reduced to nine, due to a different distribution of contents that coordinated them with the order of presentation found in the chapters. At first, a version of canon one was proposed which anathematized simultaneously all who deny that the mass is a true and proper sacrifice, all who equate immolation with eating the body of Christ, and all who say that the eucharist benefits only those who receive communion. The emended version of the canon relegates mention of the third error to the canon which deals with propitiation.

What was first listed as canon two, and then moved to third place, draws out the meaning of what is meant by true and proper sacrifice. It condemns those who say that the mass is only a sacrifice of praise and thanksgiving, or a mere

---

[47] The Council does not say whether this is a pious belief or one that is solidly grounded in the scriptures.

commemoration of the cross, or that it cannot be offered for the living and the dead. To meet all the challenges to the true sacrificial character of the mass, the term used is *propitiatory*. This canon was put in third place in order to make room in second place for the one which anathematizes those who deny that the origin of sacrifice and priesthood is found in the words of Christ to the apostles: *Hoc facite in meam commemorationem*. This particular canon continued to be disputed by a number of bishops, led by the archbishop of Grenada, even after the final vote was taken on the decree.[48] They contended that it could hardly be said to represent a traditional and universal belief that it was at this point that Christ instituted the priesthood, whatever about the sacrifice. However, one must note that the canon intends chiefly to define that the power of the priesthood comes from Christ, not precisely the moment of its origin. The protests of the minority made good sense, but they did not touch on the substance of the canon.

Thus, three canons give the doctrinal kernel of the magisterial decisions regarding the whole controversy between catholics and reformers. The first states that the mass is a true and proper sacrifice, the second that it, along with the priesthood, is instituted by Christ, and the third that what this means is that it is a sacrifice which can be offered for the living and the dead, for sins, satisfactions, punishments and other necessities. The exact sense of all of this becomes clear when the canons are related to the decree's chapters.

The fourth canon is apologetic in nature and condemns those who say that the mass, understood in the way proposed, takes away from the sacrifice of the cross. Further explanations of how the mass relates to the cross are left to the corresponding doctrinal chapter. The remaining canons anathematize the

---

[48] Cf. CT VIII 963 37–965 5, and 954f.

opponents of the various practices that the church upholds in the face of criticism and abuse.

## Anathema

The anathemas of the Council of Trent fall on those opposing church practice as well as on those proposing erroneous doctrine. What, it needs to be asked, is the exact bearing of anathematization and how does it bear on practice as well as on belief? In an article written in 1953, Piet Fransen showed that to condemn something under anathema was not necessarily correlative with *ex cathedra* definition, as catholic theology in its listing of theological notes or qualifications had so long supposed.[49] An anathema is rather like a curse on people who are disturbing the church because of what they are propounding, or because of what they are calling into question. They are seen to disrupt true piety and belief. The anathema defends a perspective and a system, to which both beliefs and practices are inherent, supporting and corroborating each other. It does not isolate one point from another, even when naming particular issues, but it is the interrelation of diverse factors that is the concern of a decree that enforces its viewpoint with anathemas.

At the same time, Fransen points out in the article cited that everything that falls under anathema, however practical it seems, is thought to have some doctrinal bearing, because some belief lies behind the practice, or is given concrete expression in it. This way of understanding the anathemata of Trent corroborates what has been said about the need to take doctrine and discipline as an organic whole in considering Trent's decree on the sacrifice of the mass. If one fails to keep this connection, but tries to separate the doctrine from the practice, one can no longer deal constructively with the meaning of the Council and

[49] Piet Fransen, 'Réflexions sur l'anathème au Concile de Trente', *Ephemerides Theologicae Lovaniensis* XXIX (1953) 657–672.

with its contribution to eucharistic belief and practice as a whole. As far as this decree is concerned, the main point of all the definitions is that the mass celebrated by a duly ordained priest, under whatever circumstances, is beneficial for those for whom it is offered, and that through this offering some grace of remission of sin flows. If this is not admitted, then it was apparently the idea of the Conciliar Fathers that the whole belief in the mass and the whole practice of the mass would fall apart. In a variety of ways, they endeavoured to insert this persuasion into a fuller teaching on the mass, and were very careful about its relation to the sacrifice of the cross, but none of this can hide the central issue of priestly offering.

## Reform Decrees

When we complement the decree on the mass with those positions taken by the Council of Trent in strictly disciplinary or reform decrees, we find that there is an awareness of the abuses, or even of the holes, in the accepted system of mass practice. There is talk of legitimate, necessary or desirable change in the practice of bishops, priests and faithful alike. As already noted, by the time the bishops came to formulating the definitive decree on the mass, they had come to see the participation of the faithful in the mass by communion as most desirable, and this was one of the practical reforms sought by disciplinary measures taken elsewhere in the Council. From the study of other decrees, we also know that they had seen some possibility, whatever the *non expedit* of the time, for the use of the vernacular and the extension of the chalice to the laity.[50] This meant that, however much latin could be exalted as the language of mystery and unity, not all could rest content with the thought that the people remained ignorant spectators of

[50] Cf. John M. Huels, 'Trent and the Chalice: Forerunner of Vatican II?', *Worship* 56 (1982) 386–400.

what goes on at mass. It meant also that, however much what were in fact private masses could be dubbed public because of the minister who celebrated, or however much celebration by a priest without communion of the faithful could be justified, not all were satisfied with the practice of communion once or twice a year.

As far as necessary changes in the mass system were concerned, the Council turned its attention to the correction of abuses in the celebration of mass during its final session. A list of abuses was drawn up by an appointed group. The list included such things as two priests celebrating mass at adjacent altars, or even at the one altar, what were called dry masses, substituting masses for the dead for Sunday propers, and the practice of masses said in a prescribed sequence, of which the best known to us today is the series called Gregorian masses.[51] All of these were looked upon as ways in which priests could increase their revenues from the mass, and as things that encouraged superstition. It was considered legitimate to connect alms to the priest for his sustenance with the application of the mass for specific persons, but the mass should not be turned to gainful employment.

In the end, this list of abuses was not promulgated or condemned in a formal decree, but the Council officially registered only a fairly mild statement. Josef Jungmann summarizes its content as follows:

The *Decretum de observandis et evitandis in celebratione missae*,[52] which was passed on September 17, 1562, in the twenty-second session, as a supplement to the teaching and the canons regarding the Sacrifice of the Mass, is concerned only with the most obvious abuses and evil conditions which could be lined up with the notions of avarice, irreverence and superstition. The bishops

[51] The abuses are listed CT VIII 926–928.
[52] CT VIII 962–963.

should be vigilant about stipends. Mass should be celebrated only in consecrated places. Disturbing and irreverent conduct and frivolous music must be banished. The capriciousness of priests regarding rites and prayers at Mass, and the superstitious observance of numbers for fixed Masses would have to cease.[53]

From all of this, one sees that steps were taken to encourage the laity's participation in the mass. Subsequent to the Council, more could have been done had doors not been closed by Roman authorities that the Council had left open. It is useful to recall this today when further changes are discussed and practices agreeable to all christian churches are sought and encouraged. It is also clear that the Council wanted more control on the way in which the mass was used by priests or requested by people. On this score, the Roman authorities acted more energetically, and so did many local bishops, even if things like the Gregorian masses were allowed to continue and still remain part of many a priest's repertory. However, there was an intrinsic limitation set to the church's self-criticism. This was the desire to keep the system as such and to uphold the role of the priest as minister of the sacrifice. Any change desired or prescribed had to respect this fundamental principle.

## Conclusions

When catholics engaged in ecumenical dialogue today look back to the Council of Trent, they can find evidence that the Council placed the mass in a sacramental relationship to the sacrifice of the cross. The theology of fruits which seemed to speak of the mass as an offering of the body and blood of Christ made by the church, in subordination to, but over and above, the sacrifice of Christ on the cross, was not the majority opinion of theologians or bishops at the Council. Certainly, it was not

---

[53] Josef Jungmann, *The Mass of the Roman Rite: its Origin and Development*, vol. 1 (New York: Benziger 1951) 134-135.

the view of things written into the conciliar decrees. Though it was not condemned, what was said was more favourable to a sacramental view of eucharistic sacrifice. In this sense, the pursuit of the notion of anamnesis or sacramental sacrifice as a notion that unites members of different churches is in line with the teaching of Trent.

In the second place, they can rightly note that though the Council of Trent strongly approved the offering of mass for the living and the dead, it did not embrace any particular theory of efficacy to explain this tradition. The theologians argued about efficacy *ex opere operato*, by way of analogy with sacramental efficacy for those receiving the sacraments, and about efficacy *per modum suffragii*, but the conciliar fathers adopted a generic and circumspect way of speaking that would defend the practice, without offering any theoretical explanation of it. In this respect, to say that the catholic theology of propitiation for the dead means intercession for the dead, as the Lima report does, contradicts nothing defined at Trent, but embraces one side of the discussion that took place there.

In the third place, catholics could point out that with all the discussions about the definition and nature of sacrifice, and despite the heavy emphasis on propitiation, Trent took no stand on how thanksgiving and propitiation are related to one another. The bias of the time, on the protestant as well as on the catholic side, separated the propitiation by which redemption was won from the thanksgiving to be offered for it in the mass. For this reason, much of the discussion had to do with whether or not Christ could be rightly offered in the mass after the consecration which recalled and represented his sacrifice of propitiation. However, the debates show that some had thought about a closer link between thanksgiving and propitiation, but were not in a position to find an answer to the question, given the reigning theology of consecration and the general ignorance about the form and origin of the eucharistic prayer. It is therefore quite possible to pursue this question further today, on the basis of fresh insights, without contradicting Trent.

In the fourth place, a comparable impasse seemed to have been reached when theologians and bishops raised the question about the relation of the mass to last supper, resurrection and heavenly intercession, alongside the question of its relation to the cross. The theology of redemption at the time was so heavily concentrated on the cross that the place of Christ's other acts in redemption was not well worked out. Naturally, this led to problems in explaining the signified of the eucharist. That the matter is still not totally resolved is apparent from the positions noted in the Lima report, but once again it can be said that Trent is not contradicted if the eucharist's sacramental meaning is further explored.

While these four conclusions help us to rise above some of the controversial issues of the sixteenth century, it is not possible to pass over the fact of Trent's central concern with the role of the priest in the offering of the mass. Whether the Council expressed its relation to the cross, or whether it defended its offering for the living and the dead, it was the sacramental act of the priest that it had in mind. This therefore remains a crux of ecumenical agreement and an issue for catholics when they relate present catholic thought to the Council of Trent. In the Lutheran/Roman Catholic dialogue, as noted, the catholic party tried to get over the difficulty about the church offering Christ by offering an apologetic for this that would not add any merit to Christ's original offering on the cross in this act. The lutheran party, however, made explicit mention of the problems that existed in the sixteenth century over the role of the priest, indicating that some of these remain, so long as catholics continue with certain practices that flow from the Tridentine view of the priestly ministry. No response has ever been offered to this in ecumenical agreements, but Pope John Paul II has on several occasions chosen to reaffirm, and indeed to strengthen, Trent's position, while the Congregation for the Doctrine of the Faith in its observations on the ARCIC report drew attention to the way in which it by-passed this issue. In short, while a theology of the eucharist as memorial sacrifice, or in a more general sense as anamnesis of Christ's mysteries, can offer a viewpoint of sacramentality that is acceptable to different christian confessions, the risk is that in the same words they may be talking about different things, and that the beliefs embodied in different practices may still be quite far apart. When these are doctrinally explicitated, as in the words of John Paul II, the depth of the difference that remains becomes apparent. On the other hand, if catholics wish to change these practices now, and to situate the priest in a relation to the community that differs from that expressed at Trent, they need to work out the attitudes to be taken to those definitions and decrees when context and thought have changed.

# Appendix

This schema is offered to help make the issue clearer.

| Categories | Trent | Agreed Statements | John Paul II |
|---|---|---|---|
| Propitiation | Same priest & victim, offering for sin. | Offering Christ. Self-offering with him. Intercession for living & dead. | Offering for sin. |
| Representation of cross | Same priest & victim. Power to offer from Xt. | Effective memorial. | Sacramental offering of priest in persona Christi. |
| Offering | Christ through priest. Priest offers mass. Spiritual offering of non-communicants. Communion participation in fruits of sacr. | Thanksgiving. Offering Christ. Self-offering in union with Christ. | Sacramental offering of priest. Spiritual offering of congregation. Communion participation in fruits. |

|  |  |  |  |
| --- | --- | --- | --- |
| Sacrifice | Propitiation. Representation of XT's death. Consecration & oblation. | Thanksgiving memorial. Effective proclamation. Christ's death. Cumulative work of redemption. Total celebration. | Propitiatory sacrifice of death. Words and acts of supper repeated by priest. |
| Priest | Power from Christ. Instrument of Christ. Church's public minister | Presides over celebration of church. | In persona Christi |
| Faithful | Spiritual offering. Fruits of sacrifice through communion. | Body of Christ which celebrates and keeps memorial. | Spiritual offering. Fruits through communion. |
| Practice | Priestly cult, public & private. Religious system. | Liturgical memorial in community. | Priestly cult for church, active participation of people. |

## Chapter 5

## DOGMA AND ITS INTERPRETATION

In the statements that result from ecumenical dialogue and in
recent pronouncements of the Roman magisterium, there are
sundry attempts to incorporate the teaching of Trent on the
sacrifice of the mass into a new ecclesial context. The first set of
statements show a desire to overcome the divisions of the
sixteenth century, so as to establish doctrinal and practical
foundations for a united community of believers. The Roman
statements are attentive to the liturgical changes that came with
the aftermath of the Second Vatican Council but try to integrate
the active participation of the faithful into a priestly system,
which in substance remains virtually identical with the
Tridentine perception of priesthood and its relation to the
church. Indeed, one might say that the price of the recognition
of the laity's part in the eucharist is an even stronger sacralization
of the priesthood than one finds in the teachings of the Council
of Trent.

Both attempts constitute a reinterpretation and what is now
called a re-reception of an older dogma into the historical
present of the catholic communion. In recent years, the
foremost examples of re-reception of dogma are found in
attitudes to the Council of Chalcedon and in attitudes to the
definition of the papal primacy at the First Vatican Council. Of
the first, Yves Congar has written:

Within the framework of present christological research, which
speaks much more of the man-Jesus of the Synoptic Gospels, one
talks of a re-reception of Chalcedon. Chalcedon remains in
possession and has not been put into question, but in a new
context of christological vision, and also of ecumenical research,

it is imperative to give a new reading of its history and of its deepest intentions, and in this way to 'receive' it anew.[1]

Of the definition of the primacy of the bishop of Rome at the First Vatican Council, it is asked how it may be received anew into an ecclesial context where the collegiality of bishops has been given firm recognition, as well as the importance in ecclesiology of each local church.[2] In that context, the meaning of the Roman primacy appears differently, and even the theological and juridical expressions of it need to change. In this second example, the deep unity between doctrine and practice is obvious.

In the case of the dogma that the mass is a sacrifice of propitiation, we see the repercussions on its re-reception of both christological and ecclesiological perspectives. If the eucharist is the sacramental memorial of the redemptive work of Christ, then the understanding of redemption and of the person of Christ has repercussions on how this work is remembered. For example, the notions of sacrifice and of satisfaction for sin that were used in medieval theology to explain the redemption were also employed to explain the mass. Fresh considerations on both these scores necessarily have results in the way that the mass is understood and celebrated. As far as ecclesiology is concerned, it is the retrieval of the local church as subject, in place of a hierarchical and institutional perception of the ordained

[1] Yves Congar, 'La 'Réception' comme réalité ecclésiologique', Revue des Sciences Philosophiques et Théologiques 56 (1972) 375: 'Dans le cadre des recherches christologiques présentes, qui parlent beaucoup plus de l'homme-Jésus des Synoptiques, on a parlé de "re-réception" de Chalcédoine. Chalcédoine est acquis et n'est pas mis en question, mais dans un nouveau contexte de vision christologique, et aussi de recherche oecuménique, on doit procéder à une nouvelle lecture de son histoire et de ses intentions profondes et ainsi le "recevoir" de nouveau.'

[2] Cf. H. Pottmeyer, 'Continuità e innovazione nell'ecclesiologia del Vaticano II', in L'Ecclesiologia del Vaticano II: Dinamismi e Prospettive, a cura di G. Alberigo (Bologna: Ed. Dehoniane 1981) 71–95.

ministry, that has greatest theological and practical consequences for the eucharist. The intent of the dogma, namely, to give the church the sacramental means to unite itself in faith with the mystery of the cross, remains the same, but the ecclesial and christological consciousness of the church, in a new set of historical conditions, is not the same.

To put the dogma of Trent in perspective, and to receive it anew according to the meaning and sense of the church today, it is helpful to see it: (a) as the historically conditioned expression of the *meaning* of the church's sacramental communion in Christ's cross; (b) as a form of language that united the doctrinal and practical interests of the church's *worship*; (c) as a language that is subject to the objective and subjective *limitations of the historical period* to which it belongs; (d) as the corporate and social quest for the basic *imperatives of faith* that pertain to eucharistic celebration in the church, which, whatever the dogma's temporal conditioning, remain of fundamental inspiration at a later time. If insight can be gained into the dogma on these four counts, then it may be possible to retrieve its basic meaning and impulse in such a way that it serves the church today in its renewal of eucharistic doctrine and practice.

## Dogma as Meaning[3]

Catholic theology for too long operated on the basis of the assumption that there can be adequate correspondence between reality and what the human person knows about reality. Doctrines and dogmas could then be taken as unchanging expressions of revealed truth and mystery. What theology ignored in this approach was the difference between faith and understanding, and between mystery and what is understood of it. Too little attention was paid likewise to the inseparability of the world of thinking from the world of feeling, and along with

[3] Cf. Bernard Lonergan, *Method in Theology* (London: DLT 1971) 295–334.

this the interpenetration of the doctrinal and the practical orders. Furthermore, little account was taken of the intersubjective quality of all knowledge and practice, and the historical conditioning of what is lived and how it is explained. Doctrine and dogma are however inserted into this complex network. One way of taking account of this is to say that dogma expresses meaning, that is to say, the lived and at least incipiently theoretical approach to the truths of faith that guides a church in its quest for communion with God in Jesus Christ. As so formulated, meaning is related to the mystery that is sought but is not taken as though it were a perfect and adequate expression of it. It is rather the embodiment in both thought and practice of the quest for truth, as lived and explained by the church at a given time, in the midst of given historical and cultural circumstances.

To say, then, that dogma is an expression of meaning is not to say that it is an adequate expression of a point of belief, as if no more were to be said on it, or as though this expression may not be superseded by another. Nor is it to infer a distinction between intellect and feeling, or between thought and practice, as though a dogma could persist even while the world of feelings and of practice is subject to change. Expressions of meaning, and search for truth, are too much tied up with feeling and practice for this to be possible. A dogmatic teaching on the part of the church, taught by the magisterium and received by the faithful, is rather a guarantee that fidelity to this particular expression of faith, in given historical circumstances, mediates the mystery of Jesus Christ and of redemption in him to believers so that they can enter into a communion of faith with God through him. It may not be the sole possible expression at that time, nor even the best possible, but it is true to the mystery of Jesus Christ and its mediation.

At the same time, to take account of dogma's meaning, the intersubjective elements, the historical conditioning, the practices to which the doctrinal expression is attached, the elements of feeling and value that give it plausibility within a culture, have to be examined. Some differentiation of mind has enabled the magisterium to distinguish between doctrinal expression and practice, so that some level of abstraction is achieved, but this is not pure or complete. The extent to which it is verified has to be looked for in the historical circumstances and discussions of the time. The choice of terms used implies a historical and conditioned judgment, for the church pronounces itself on how these are understood, on what practices they imply, on what values they embody, at the time the teaching is solemnized. As we know from the history of early trinitarian and christological controversies, there could be argument over what expressions or words ought to be used, as well as over their actual usage in definition, even when the teaching had been promulgated. What the official teaching and its use of given terms guarantees is their heuristic value as used in pronouncements. In that sense dogmatic terms can be taken as a kind of grammar of faith. If people abide by the usage that is canonized, they can pursue the knowledge of faith and theological investigation by this means. When the magisterium insists on these terms to the extent of proscribing others, that is a distinction between a grammar of faith that aids the search for truth and a grammer that can mislead.

The conciliar debates at the Council of Trent, as they have been described, and the devotional background that has been briefly evoked, make it clear that these various factors were at work in the drawing up of the doctrines and definitions. The listing of articles and canons on the sacrifice of the mass gave evidence from the very beginning that practice and doctrinal explanation were inseparably interwoven. What the Council's doctrines and dogmas explained was a way of worshipping, that took the mediation of the ordained priest as an essential factor in the celebration of the sacramental memorial of Christ's death.

Not only was it essential, but a particular way of exercising this ministry was at the heart of a whole devotional system, so that all of Trent's teaching on the eucharistic memorial and sacrifice took this for granted, and took it as the key factor to be defended. Left without this form of priesthood, it seemed as though the catholic faithful would be left without the possibility of benefiting from Christ's once and for all sacrifice. Historians of the post-reformation period of the church's life have pointed to the difficulties that the reformers encountered in implementing their alternative models of worship and teaching, or have even described the kind of superstition into which people could fall back who were deprived of the catholic mass and did not take to the reformation supper, or the other forms of reformation worship.[4]

The reformers did indeed have their counterposition to the medieval ecclesial, religious and liturgical system. There is no guarantee of any sort that the bishops of the Council of Trent, as advised by the theologians, understood what the reformation sought or what this system was. It is all too clear that they did not sympathize with it, as it is clear that the reformers often attacked what was base in the medieval system, without taking account of its positive values. While defining a catholic model of eucharistic practice by anathema, the Council proscribed what it understood as alternative models. This was to say that within the context of the time they were misleading, created a disturbance of faith and devotion, and so were harmful to the church and to its belief. That this could be the case, or was at times the case, history would affirm. That it had to be the case, or was always the case, history would deny. However, the direct object of the conciliar teaching and explanation was the catholic system. This it presented as a legitimate model for practice, as one in keeping with apostolic tradition, and one that

[4] Cf. Steven Ozment, *The Age of Reform 1250–1550* 436.

when properly explained denied nothing to Christ's redemption, but proved an efficacious way of mediating its graces to the living and the dead. What the conciliar participants did not apparently perceive was how historically conditioned both the practical and doctrinal elements of the system were.

Today, we cannot retrieve and integrate the interests of the conciliar position on the mass without this awareness, especially as it affects the role of the priest in church and sacrament. Church institution and church worship are both integral to the meaning system whereby an ecclesial community enters into a communion of faith with God in Jesus Christ. Though the ministry of word and sacrament must always have a place in the church, and though they cannot be performed without being incorporated into effective institutional forms, it would seem that this can be done in a variety of ways without breaking historical continuity and communion in the one faith and worship. To say this is but to take account of the divergent cultural perceptions that affect the way of living faith, and the different ways that there are of reckoning with the elements of gospel and tradition that are vital to christian life.

To say, therefore, with the Council of Trent, that the mediatorship of divine presence and grace practised by the priest within the medieval sacramental system was the means whereby the sacramental memorial of the death of Christ was realized, or to say that this can still be efficacious today, with whatever modifications of the system deemed culturally desirable, is not to say that the role of the ordained ministry may not assume a different mode of mediating communion in the eucharistic memorial. In particular, when we read the teaching of Trent that through the act of the priest in celebrating mass, whether with or without communicants, forgiveness of sins is mediated and shared between the living and the dead, this may raise important issues about a communion in grace through public worship, but it does not have to mean that alternative models of ministry and of communion in forgiveness and grace are not possible, or that this cannot be meaningfully worked out in a different set of cultural conditions. This pursuit of a new embodiment of meaning cannot even be denied the catholic community. Still less can Trent be taken as an imperative for the modelling of culturally and ecclesially apt forms of ministry and worship in other churches. Given the intersubjectivity of a church whose members were party to a classically hierarchical perception of reality and of divine presence, to have tampered with this form of ministry and worship may have had repercussions injurious to faith and piety, and to follow this system was indeed a medium whereby communion in the death of Christ was assured to many, contrary to the accusations levelled too globally against it by the reformers. However, to be intransigent about its maintenance is to give it a value that presumes to transcend the cultural and historical conditions that affect the church's doctrine and practice. The examination offered of the way in which the system evolved and of the tridentine discussions would seem to eliminate this possibility, if indeed it is not excluded by the very nature of human meaning. Dogma is never a purely abstract expression of truth, but it is always the historically conditioned mode whereby a subject, to wit a church community, seeks a way of communion with the God revealed in Jesus Christ. It does not stand alone, but belongs within an entire system of things that together constitute meaning.

Basic to the position attributed to the priest in this system is the meaning given to worship itself. The order of worship is one in which offering is preferred to thanksgiving. It is seen as the most fundamental act of religion. Propitiation has to be made for sin by an offering, and from a catholic perspective the offering of a gift seems a necessary precedent to the receiving of a greater one. The only worthy propitiation that can be offered is Christ himself, but this needed to be integrated into a religious system in which the propitiation is continually offered. There were moments in the practice and theology of the church when this seemed to be an offering made by the church, but in their better moments both made it clear that the offering in question was Christ's own sacramental offering, now made available to the church so that it could share in it. However, what is always to the fore in the system is that religion of its nature requires the primacy of offering, and that this religious need is met and perfected in the catholic liturgy, through the eucharistic sacrifice.

The Reformers, on the other hand, took the free gift of grace as the central point of an order of worship. They by no means excluded the demand on believers to make of themselves a self-offering, in communion with Christ, but they wished neither the offering of gifts nor the offering of Christ by the church to be at the heart of worship. That heart could be nothing other than the free gift of the divine mercy won by the death of Christ, the once and for all offering or sacrifice of redemption. Hence both in the sixteenth century and now, reformation churches do not wish to make any mention of offering Christ in the eucharist, since even when explained as a union in the sacramental memorial of the cross it suggests an approach to worship that diminishes the gratuity of grace.

That the meaning given to faith in these two systems of worship is different seems clear enough. That they are in fundamental opposition to one another, or that either one has to be rejected as incompatible with the gospel, would seem to be open to question. Perhaps what we need to see today in ecumenical dialogue is that faith in the saving death and resurrection of Christ can be appropriated through and in worship in systemically different ways, and that there is no single absolute order of worship or absolute eucharistic theology.

Sociological studies, especially those that concentrate on

popular piety and local religion, indicate that a fuller grasp of how faith is expressed through meaning would require that the catholic dogma and protestant reform would both need to be seen in relation to social change and social ordering. This is an arduous study, depending in great measure on the success of local histories, so that only a brief indication of what it implies can be given here. The fundamental perception is that faith in Christ is assimilated to the way in which a believing people orders society, or seeks to change that order, in the face of new interests and in the light of new faith perceptions. In line with this fundamental perception, it can be pointed out that the ordering of worship as sacrifice and the ordering of worship as sacrament of gift and grace relate to two different perceptions of the social order. The ordering of worship as sacrifice reflects the desire to bring a diversified society into unity, to overcome divisions and distinctions, even while they remain, by an expression of ultimate oneness in Christ and in surrender to God. A medieval society which lived by a division of the populace into social ranks, and which perceived the total order of things as one which united the faithful of heaven, purgatory and earth, could find its spiritual unity, and even its temporal unity, in the act of sacrifice. On the other hand, the ordering of worship as sacrament reflects a perception of society which starts with the fundamental fellowship of all in the grace of Christ, and in this unity of sacrament sees the model of a social order to be constructed. It is less prone to sanction the hierarchical rankings of social or ecclesial order, and more attuned to the ordering of society as the work of all the people. That the grace of Christ prevails over this ordering is expressed in the gratuity of sacrament, that it is an ordering in which all participate in the equality of their common calling is expressed by an ordering of worship around the images of the holy fellowship and the common table of the Lord's Supper.

When this relation of eucharistic worship to the share of

christians in ordering the common good of humanity is taken into account, we can see that our own present ordering of the eucharist will be differentiated from sixteenth century models. When dogma is looked at as meaning, we perceive a number of things. First, we see that practice and doctrine are reciprocal in their interaction and cannot be considered separately. Secondly, we see that to be lived faith has to be constituted as meaning, and that dogma is an expression of the meaning through which people at a given time live in faith. Thirdly, we see that different orderings of meaning are possible, and can be viewed both positively and critically in such a way that their apparent oppositions are overcome, without pretence however of reducing them to finally saying the same thing. Fourthly, we see that no ordering of worship can be comprehensively understood without some awareness of how it relates to the participation of worshippers in the making of the social order.

## Dogma as Worship

In some recent writings, several theologians have explored the relation of dogma to worship.[5] For one thing, the idea that worship is a kind of *theologia prima*, as distinct from the *theologia secunda* of reflective theology, has gained considerable acceptance.[6] For another, there is a growing realization that worship as the act of a community is a kind of canon within which dogmatic and theological issues are subjected to the discernment of faith.[7] In the third place, it is acknowledged that

[5] E. Schlink, 'Die Struktur der dogmatischen Aussage als ökumenisches Problem', *Kerygma und Dogma* 3 (1957) 251–306; W. Pannenberg, 'Analogie und Doxologie' in W. Joest and W. Pannenberg (eds.), *Dogma und Denkstrukturen* (Göttingen: Vandenhoeck & Ruprecht 1963) 96–115; G. Wainwright, *Doxology: The Praise of God in Worship, Doctrine and Life* (Oxford & New York: Oxford University Press 1980) 251–283.

[6] G. Lukken, 'La liturgie comme lieu théologique irremplacable', *Questions Liturgiques et Paroissiales* 56 (1975) 97–112.

[7] Harvey Guthrie, *Theology as Thanksgiving: From Israel's Psalms to the Church's Eucharist* (New York: Seabury 1981) 181–216.

the act of faith expressed in acts of worship attains the object of faith in a way that doctrines and theologumena do not.[8] In the fourth place, some have asked whether all dogma does not have to be explicitly related to the worship from which it springs and to which it intends, at least implicitly, to give support.[9]

It is the fourth point that merits particular consideration here, since it has special importance for an interpretation of the Tridentine positions on the sacrifice of the mass. Some parallel can be drawn between this interpretation and the interpretation of christological dogmas offered by Frans Van Beeck in his book *Christ Proclaimed: Christology as Rhetoric*.[10] He proposes that these dogmas are intended to draw believers into right worship, and that hence they are to be studied as a particular form of rhetoric. He describes rhetoric as follows:

> Rhetoric is the sum of all those elements and aspects of language which show that language is primarily an activity in situations and only on that basis a cognitive act; it is language insofar as it is evidence of, and incentive to, persons' active communication with one another in particular situations; it is language insofar as it bears traces of worldly situations being places for personal encounter and interaction, in which the experience of the 'other' also becomes an experience of transcendence; it is language insofar as it is marked by the process of change brought about by interpersonal encounter and orientation to transcendence; it is language insofar as it evinces the *process* of intelligent articulation of these experiences of situation, encounter, transcendence and change.[11]

[8] Aidan Kavanagh, *On Liturgical Theology* (New York: Pueblo 1984) 122–150.

[9] This point is made in Faith and Order Paper No. 103, *Spirit of God, Spirit of Christ: Ecumenical Reflections on the Filioque Controversy* (London: SPCK, and Geneva: WCC 1981) 10.

[10] Frans Van Beeck, *Chrst Proclaimed: Christology as Rhetoric* (New York: Paulist 1979).

[11] op. cit. 101.

If we apply this definition of rhetoric to the dogma of Trent on the sacrifice of the mass, we can see how it is an attempt to address a changing ecclesial situation. At first, the history of the debates during the Council suggests that the members of the synod were sluggish in admitting change, or in dealing with change, or even that they were resisting it. Nonetheless, as we compare the initial debates of 1547 with the final decree of 1562, we can see the process whereby the Council has dealt with change, moving with and stemming the tide at one and the same time. On the one hand, we see how some clarifications served the purpose of true worship. In particular, one can think of how the relation of the mass to the cross was clarified in such a way in the course of the Council as to exclude all possibility of conceiving of two distinct sacrifices, or of how the Council's position on the role of the priest was modified at least to the degree that communion of the faithful was taken to be their normal participation in the sacrifice. On the other hand, it would seem that certain historical opportunities were missed, largely due to failure in establishing an adequate intersubjective relation in the situation of change between reformers and catholics. Opposition took the place of dialogue, with the result that there were two opposing rhetorics. This did not stop the process of change, but shaped it in such a way that oppositions were built into the course of history. It also had an effect on catholic thought that made it doubly resistant to certain features of change. For example, the community as such was not allowed its role as primary subject in eucharistic celebration. Instead, the priest as public minister remained the subject that worshipped, and the community could only be a secondary subject, in total subordination to him.

As qualities of dogma perceived as rhetoric, Van Beeck notes that it is a language of obedience and a language of inclusion. This is not an *a priori* totally positive assessment of all dogmatic teaching. It is rather a view of the basic intent of dogma, and in fact offers a further development of critical judgment, since it means that we can consider dogma historically in terms of how successfully it realized this dual purpose. As language of inclusion, dogma's intent is to include all persons and all human situations, to pursue the identification of the christian with the human, so that nothing and no one is excluded from the communion of love and transcendence. As language of obedience, it wishes to submit all to the lordship of Jesus Christ, to bring the superabundant grace of his redemption to all persons and situations.

We can see this double intent operative in Trent's discussion and teaching in two ways. First of all, the conciliar fathers explained the worship, priesthood and sacrifice of the gospel by way of comparison with the worship, priesthood and sacrifice of the natural law and of the old law. The basic thrust behind this seems to have been the vision that all things human are redeemed and fulfilled in Christ, and that human nature with all its tendencies is saved in him. Looked at critically, the debate and the decree show deficiencies in an understanding of the religious and in a perception of the relation of the gospel and the sacraments of the gospel to nature and to the old law. However, this does not mean that the intent of what was said and done can be ignored. Inspired today by the remembrance of Trent, the church must continue to look for the ways in which the human quest for the transcendent is to be incorporated into the eucharistic memorial.

Secondly, much of the differences between the reformers and the catholics had to do with inclusion. Both would admit that all the living and all the dead who are saved in Christ are gathered into one communion of grace. What the Tridentine fathers wanted to defend was a particular mode of worship, namely, the priest's offering of the mass for persons not present, both the living and the dead, which they saw as an expression of this communion in grace and the forgiveness of sin. Finding apt ways whereby to explain this gave them no little trouble, as has been seen from the history of the debate, but it remained something that they saw fit to retain, even while in the end offering a minimum of explanation. As the agreement between lutherans and catholics in 1978 states, account has to continue to be taken in the practice and understanding of the mass of this communion in grace and the forgiveness of sin that transcends the particular congregation gathered in an act of worship. It is not necessarily the particular expression, which is the priestly application of mass, that is to be kept, but the intent of the definition must still be met, according to new perspectives and ways of worship.

## Dogma and Symbol: Limitation of Language

Since rhetoric appeals to the affective and not merely to the intellectual, to the communitarian and not to the isolated individual, to value and not merely to the factual, to the intent of the transcendent and not merely to understanding of the given, it has to be a language that is symbolic. One of the criticisms levelled against dogma, and particularly against the catholic dogma that followed the reform, is that it is a quest for understanding that has lost touch with its roots in the symbolic, and in the experiential which is brought to expression and transformed through symbol.[12] This is not to say that symbols are not used in dogma, but that when they are used they are given a conceptual content that reduces the potential for meaning of the original symbol. This is a reduction of both its cognitive and affective power. What has happened in the course of time to the symbol of original sin is a good illustration of this

[12] Cf. Eric Voegelin, *The Ecumenic Age*, vol. 4 of *Order and History* (Baton Rouge: Louisiana State University Press 1974) 58, and Matthew Lamb, *Solidarity With Victims: Toward a Theology of Social Transformation* (New York: Crossroad 1982) 101f.

process. It is a term which derives from narrative and other forms of imaginative discourse, which are addressed to the experience of sin that englobes human consciousness and human life. When placed, however, in a doctrinal context its roots with the poetic texts wherein it has birth is largely lost. Hence it is made to stand for a set of ideas and concepts rather than for a world of meaning in which psychic roots and affective intent take their place alongside the cognitive. Clarity of thought and the attempt to give an unassailable account of the origins of sin in human history is substituted for those expressions that allow us to give voice to the awareness of the extent to which sin envelops our existence and to our need for divine mercy and grace if the human situation is to be saved from its own intrinsic distortion.

Some terms that occur in the Tridentine teaching on the sacrifice of the mass clearly belong in the order of conceptualized symbols, so that they are not allowed the full play of their potential reference. Such terms are sacrifice, propitiation and satisfaction. *Satisfaction*, for example, is a term that came into the theology of redemption from a given penitential system, but the penitential system was influenced by an order of justice that relied for the stability of order on the rendering of penalties for breaches of the law, and also allowed for a commutation of penalties. Its meaning lies in the sense of human relations that grounds it, and in the ordering of society that it serves. However, when introduced into a dogmatic setting it is made to stand for a notion of divine justice and for a concept of sin that is practically equated with an injury done to divine honour and right, and as far as the mass is concerned for a very practical system of making reparation and reducing sin's consequences.

The limitations inherent to the Tridentine teaching on the mass, because of this use of conceptual symbol, are manifold. The major ones can be listed.

(1) The word *sacrifice* was allowed to dominate all explanation of the eucharist as a celebration.

(a) This meant first of all that other images that could capture the meaning of the celebration were not given enough consideration. Images of the eucharist as eschatological banquet, passover, food and drink, were used in the decree on the sacrament of the eucharist, but not in the decree on the sacrifice. Only those parts of the mass which responded to the concept of offering or sacrifice, such as the consecration and the oblation that followed it, were taken into account. The conjunction of the rhetoric of sacrifice with practices such as the silent canon, the use of latin, the private mass, and the acceptance by the priest of mass-offerings, allowed for an understanding of the mass in very narrow terms.

(b) Not only did the conceptual symbol of sacrifice affect the explanation of the rite of the mass, but it also affected the remembrance of the death, of which it is the sacramental representation. In other words, references to the death of Christ risked being reduced to images of a meritorious and satisfactory offering to the Father. Other images, such as redemption, victory over death, the entry into the heavenly sanctuary through the shedding of blood, or the figures of the martyr, eschatological prophet and judge, whereby the death of Christ may be significantly remembered, were either not taken up or were totally subordinated to the conceptual symbol of sacrifice.

(2) The image of *sacrifice* was itself not given the full range of its potential reference and meaning.

(a) Primacy was given to propitatory sacrifice. Other types of sacrifice, such as thanksgiving or peace-offering, when mentioned, were dubbed secondary. Though occasional suggestions were made in the debates as to how to integrate the different aspects of the eucharist typified by reference to different kinds of sacrifice, the official teaching was stated in such a way that it seemed to register opposition instead of harmony between a theology of the mass as thanksgiving and a theology of the mass as propitiation.

(b) Propitiatory sacrifice and expiatory sacrifice were identified as one type of sacrifice. This meant that it was the need to make satisfaction to God for sin that was high-lighted. A better grasp of the imagery of expiatory sacrifice would have allowed for the imagery of covenant and for the images of the divine initiative in granting peace and pardon. In effect, as seen, a text that spoke of the initiative of God's love and mercy was eliminated from the final version of the decree, because it was thought inconsequential to the points of controversy that the Council wished to address.

(c) Concomitant with this confusion between propitiatory and expiatory was the equation of sacrificial ritual with offering. Time and time again, definitions were offered by speakers at the Council that identified sacrifice with the offering of a victim, or a dedication to God by consecration. This meant that in the typology of sacrifice that was the Council's reference point, attention was not given to other parts of sacrificial ritual, such as the sprinkling with blood (unless it was equated with immolation of offering), the recitative of God's mighty deeds, and the prayer of memorial. Even communion was mentioned only as a participation in the fruits of sacrifice.

(d) Nor was there any appreciation at the Council of the metaphorical use of words and the power of metaphor. The tendency at that time was to see the real and the metaphorical as mutually exclusive, or to take the metaphorical as only a linguistic device, intended to illustrate some points of doctrine. The transferred use of the language of sacrifice, taken from ritual, to the lives of the faithful and to the death of Christ was not explored for its significance. Indeed, the reformers and their catholic opponents seemed to take sacrifice in an univocal sense and hence to place an opposition between the use of the word in speaking of the faithful, since this was dubbed metaphor, and its use in speaking of Christ's death, since this was a use of the word in its real sense. Hence, the question all too often was how the mass as a rite constituted an offering. Today, it is possible to ask what is the meaning of keeping sacramental commemoration of a death that is called by a name taken from the ritual order, and whose meaning is expressed by references to the multiple ritual action, including offering, but not reducible to offering.

(e) In using the concept of offering to explain the mass, the Tridentine fathers and theologians tended to restrict its meaning to that part of the mass which comprised the institution narrative and its immediate aftermath. In this way, they lost touch with the early liturgical tradition which included the entire action, as a gathering and act of the congregation of faith and love, within this term.

### Dogma and the Imperatives of Faith[13]

In looking at Trent's teaching on the sacrifice of the mass, even while aware of its historical limitations, can we see what positive guidelines it still offers in the quest for sound teaching and sound eucharistic practice? The dogma belongs to the church today, only if it is seen, not as an abstract statement of truth, but as an action taken by a corporate body, which was the gathering of bishops, theologians, and some lay persons, at the Council, acting on behalf of a fuller corporate body, which was the church, and in the interests of the belief and practice of the church. Furthermore, the Council's action has to be taken as something that could be effective only as received into the life of the church. It is best to avoid the abstract question as to whether or not the truth of dogma holds *ex sese* or *ex consensu ecclesiae*, and to consider it in the process of its being defined in relation to

[13] Lamb, op. cit. The operation suggested by Lamb in relating dogma to the transforming imperatives of faith is much vaster than what is attempted here, since it would require attention to political and economic factors. However, the inspiration of chapter 5 of this book is acknowledged.

church life and being received into church life. Its reception into the life of the corporate subject of the church is clearly essential to the meaning that it had and has in the life of the church, whatever about the abstract question of its initial truth.

Dogma's relation to the total ecclesial reality is addressed by Matthew Lamb when he writes of a dogma as a social performance. When it is considered as a social performance, then it has to be considered in relation to the persons who were involved in its evolution, as well as in relation to the persons who were affected by it, or continue to be affected by it. History looked at it in this way means 'meeting persons, appreciating the values to represent, criticizing their defects, and allowing one's life to be challenged at its very roots by their words and by their deeds'.[14] It is this encounter and challenge that is at the heart of a re-reception of dogma. In looking back to Trent, the catholic church has to consider the involvement of all believers at that time, and in this time, with what was then going on. In other words, the Tridentine position has to be seen as part of the dialectic in which believers were involved, a dialectic that engaged the reformers as much as the catholics. The church as subject in the sixteenth century was made up not only of those who remained in communion with the See of Rome, but it was all believers who adhered in faith to Jesus Christ. When catholic theologians today entertain the question about a possible catholic reception of the *Confessio Augustana*, this cannot be the fruit of an attempt to find the same thing in the Lutheran Confessions and in Trent. It means rather that a consideration of Trent as social performance means necessarily a consideration of the social performance of those with whom ecclesial communion was broken. The reception of the *Confessio Augustana*, or of other reformation confessions, and the re-reception of Trent are two parts of the one basic question about

[14] Lonergan, op. cit. 247.

the relation of eucharistic doctrine and practice today to the eucharistic doctrine and practice of the time of schism. Since it is a specifically catholic enquiry, the immediate concern in this book is with the ways in which the imperatives of faith and practice were expressed by the Council of Trent. At the same time, this cannot be properly appreciated except in relation to the questions put by the reformers, the insights that they expressed and that were not appreciated on the catholic side, and to the failure to overcome historical impasse.

The way in which we engage with the past and its challenge is shaped by current insights, perspectives and historical conditions. In listing a number of points from the Council of Trent, the major interest is in the retrieval of the local community as subject of ecclesial action and identity. This seems to be the vital élan of current ecclesiology, sacramentology and ecclesial practice, as catholic communities attend to the openness to Word, Spirit and historical reality that was fundamental to the experience and teaching of the Second Vatican Council, and in which they often find themselves partner to the experience and interests of other christian churches.[15] The fundamental eucharistic question, then, is how a community of believers, united in the Spirit, keeps memorial of the death of Jesus Christ, what structures of order and celebration are the most apt in doing this, and what effect this has on the social and apostolic reality of the community, as sacrament of Christ's presence and of the power of the Spirit in the world.

With all of this in mind, the following observations can be made about the pertinence of the dogma on the sacrifice of the mass as social performance to current ecclesial interests, sacramental practice and doctrinal expression.

[15] Cf. Antonio Acerbi, 'Receiving Vatican II in a Changed Historical Context', *Concilium* 146 (English edition; New York & Edinburgh: Seabury and T. & T. Clark 1981) 77–84.

(1) Trent recognized the importance of relating its teaching on the eucharist, as well as its practice, to both Scripture and Tradition. Limits and biases are evident in the way that it went about this, both on the relation of scripture and tradition to one another and to the living church, and on the early practice of the eucharist. However, it remains a concrete and practical example of a historical church resolving its practical and doctrinal issues in this way.

(2) In face of some catholic extremes, in both practice and theology, the Council was faithful to the imperative of relating the mass to the cross of Christ in harmonious unity, so that nothing would take from the cross's sufficiency, and no human merit would intervene between Christ's saving grace and the sinner. Whatever inadequacies showed up in the use of terms, the rhetoric of commemoration and representation was kept as central to the explanation and practice of the eucharist. The very fact that various theories were put forward to explain this relation, and that not being able to choose between them the Council in its official pronouncement remained quite general, is itself an instigation to keep this question alive and to probe it further, as resources permit.

(3) In the given historical circumstances of the time, Trent assured that the language and imagery of sacrifice would not fall into the oblivion of dead metaphor or allegory, and that it would remain attached to the central act of the eucharist, rather than being relegated to something that seemed secondary. We can of course only regret that thanksgiving was taken to be a secondary aspect of the eucharistic sacrifice, but it is clear that at the time for catholics to have used sacrificial terminology only in relation to thanksgiving or to the life of the faithful would have meant that they would have ceased to ask the question why sacrificial language was adopted as central to the sacramental memorial of the sacrificial death of Christ. Of course, in conjunction with this we are sensitive to the reformation allergy

to a use of sacrificial language which seemed at times to give the mass status as independent sacrifice. In relating this whole question today to experience and to the basis of doctrine in experience, we are in a position to probe the symbolic value of this language of sacrifice in ways that were not possible at the time of the reformation, and in ways that cast light both on the meaning of the eucharist and on its celebration.

(4) The Council's teaching and advocacy kept people alert to the idea that a communion in grace and prayer is inclusive of all those reborn in Christ, both living and dead. This is not something adjacent to the eucharist, but is an intrinsic part of keeping memorial of Jesus Christ. Within the perspective of the time, Trent addressed this largely as a matter of individual needs and in the categories of satisfaction to be made for sin or intercession to be addressed for sinners. Today, with a different sense of historical communion, and with a feeling of the pertinence of a communion in faith to historical issues and social realities, we need to look for other ways in which this sense of communion with the living and the dead that is expressed in the eucharist can be understood. However, for christian faith and eucharistic practice it remains vital that the dead are not forgotten and that the hope of the eschaton engages both the living and the dead as one communion in Jesus Christ and the Spirit.

(5) That this communion between all the living, and between the living and the dead, is a communion in faith and hope in Jesus Christ was made clear by the Council in the measures that it took to assure that there would be no room for the charge of the reformers that catholic practice allowed for a remission of sins without devotion and faith on the part of the beneficiaries of the offering of the mass. The move away from theories about the mass's *ex opere operato* efficacy, and from minute calculations about the value of the mass, to more general statements is itself significant, for though these statements remained vague they at

least prevented any reductionism of mass offerings to penitential commutations. In this respect, one may say that the Council's teaching was never, up to the present, fully received by the catholic church, since much of its practice continued to be guided by an understanding of mass offerings more in tune with medieval eccentricities than with the theological caution of the Council.

(6) In choosing the definition of the mass as a sacrifice of propitiation, Trent at one and the same time illustrates the need for propitiatory language and the difficulties of dealing with it. That it itself did not come to a satisfactory resolution of the issue is as important to its reception as are its actual statements. By the end of its tenure the Council had become so circumspect on this score that it did not support the propitiatory character of the mass with the same sense of excluding other aspects that one might feel present in the earlier moments of conciliar discussion. Its interests remained thoroughly practical and in effect it found no adequate language with which to deal with the range of theoretical issues involved. It wanted above all to give its support to a given sacerdotal and institutional practice of offering mass, and to say that in as much as this represented the passion of Christ and was a public act of the church, it 'somehow' was pertinent to the forgiveness of sins. This involved no particular understanding of how the death of Christ itself mediated the forgiveness of sins, or of how this continued to be done through its sacramental memorial. In fact, *propitiatory* turns out to be one of those words that is more attached to a given practice than to a doctrinal understanding of what is involved in the practice, as well as to a particularly historically bound institutional way of mediating Christ's grace to the church. The particular meaning of the priestly act could be retained only in a church that could find given sacerdotal structures its most appropriate faith expression, and that was party to a cultural perspective that made this vision of church

possible. Reconsidering the propitiatory character of the eucharistic memorial, therefore, involves a double task. The one is a quest for church structure and a practice of ordination that is appropriate to an awareness that the community of faith is the ecclesial subject of celebration, so that the act of the ordained minister is understood in this context, rather than in the terms conjured up by the expression *public minister*. The second is to look for the ways in which forgiveness of sin and reconciliation are mediated through the celebration of the eucharist, and how this pertains not only to the communion of those who are present, but also to those not present, both living and dead. Naturally, this would mean putting the question of eucharistic reconciliation and mediation within the broader context of the church's total activity in bringing about reconciliation and in witnessing to the peace of God. Something of the interest in the *humanum* that is found in Trent's desire to find in the mass a perfect realization of natural religion would also need to be retrieved in this context, since it could be asked how the commemoration of Christ's death speaks to the role that the church has in bringing God's peace and forgiveness to all humanity, and how this corresponds to a fundamental human desire for a transcendence that heals and reconciles.

(7) It is the intersection between the role ascribed to the ordained priest and the doctrine of the sacrifice of the mass in catholic doctrine that still creates severe difficulties for other western churches. This has already been discussed and the question has been raised as to whether other expressions of ministry in the eucharist cannot be seen by the catholic church as viable options. Nonetheless, one aspect of Trent's accent on the role of the priest remains important, and that is the issue of the sacramental nature of ministry and the pertinency of this to the life of the church, inclusive of its worship. Current ecumenical dialogue shows a common concern for this sacramentality, even if it is difficult to come to an agreed proposition on it. However, both

catholics and others may see a possibility of retrieving Trent's concern when the ordained ministry is spoken of less in terms of the power that it possesses and more in terms of what it signifies and thus contributes to the life of the church and to its sacramental acts.

*Conclusion*

What has been discussed in this chapter is the need not only to know what Trent said about the mass, but to interpret it. This interpretation is done by trying to understand what its definitions meant in the broader context of the sixteenth century, and by relating this to what they might continue to mean in the very changed conditions of our time. Such interpretation is an attempt to take both the historicity and the truth of dogma seriously. Four aspects of dogma have therefore been considered in relation to the dogma defining the sacrificial nature of the mass, namely; dogma as meaning, dogma as worship, dogma as a historically conditioned language, and dogma as a historically conditioned expression of the imperatives of faith. The most serious conclusions that follow from this interpretation are the need for the catholic church to reconsider the role of the priest and the language of sacrifice on the one hand, and the possibility of doing this in a differentiated historical continuity with Trent on the other.

## Chapter 6

## THE RETRIEVAL OF PRACTICE

At the heart of the sixteenth century controversies, and at the heart of the Tridentine defence of the catholic system, lay practice. Today, it is a converging practice in liturgical worship which moves us more rapidly to mutual understanding between christian churches than do theological agreements. The recovery of the eucharistic prayer or anaphora, according to the patterns of the ancient churches, as well as the recovery of the use of the scriptures in the liturgy by the catholic church, constitute a measure of orthodoxy and orthopractice shared between churches that runs deeper than what is said on the doctrinal level. At the same time, however, it is also practice that creates the greatest obstacle to a fuller communion. By very reason of a recovery of tradition, and of the effort to formulate this in ecumenical agreement, churches are called upon to reconsider certain of their practices. Speaking from within the catholic church, the practice which seems most to stand in need of fresh consideration is that which centres on the identity of the priest and his role in the eucharist, as these continue to be affirmed by the magisterium.

A fuller knowledge of church tradition offers us the chance to draw on the past, not in order to copy it but in order to derive new potentiality from its knowledge, allied to the changes of our own time. Hence in this final chapter a brief look is offered at the broader tradition that lies prior to medieval developments that so much shaped the sixteenth century controversies. This cannot be the place to offer an exhaustive study of this eucharistic tradition, but is intended only to be indicative of what needs consideration and of what fresh possibilities are offered by way of forging and explicating a more ecumenical practice, that is at the same time sensitive to the community experience typical of this post-conciliar moment.

Two things in particular from the medieval mass system constituted the ground of dispute during the controversies of the sixteenth century, and became the primary concerns of the Tridentine defence of catholic practice and teaching. The first had to do with the possibility of offering the mass for the living and the dead, and it was with this practice that the word *propitiatory* became practically identified at Trent. The second had to do with the role of the ordained priest in offering the mass, this being closely associated with the former issue. Behind these two points lay the larger issue of the sense in which church tradition talks of the eucharist as a sacrifice, and of its relation to the sacrifice of the cross. Many of the arguments in the Tridentine debate treated the larger issue, but it was inevitably obscured because of the two points of immediate controversy.

The theologians and fathers of the Council had little trouble in showing that remembrance of the dead at the eucharist was a custom as old as Tertullian, but their arguments for the private mass that served to establish the role of the ordained priest were tortured on the one hand, and on the other based on a particular reading of Christ's relation to the apostles which cannot be scientifically upheld. In any case, when we consider the evidence of historical documents we see that the whole system of offering masses for the living and the dead, whether in suffrage or as satisfaction, and that enhancement of the role of ordination which allowed for private mass went together. This is not to say that there were not other reasons for both practices, but the point being made is that with the development of time they became inextricably interwoven, each offering some kind of justification for the other.

Consequently, if one is to establish a critical perspective on a eucharistic celebration in which the language of sacrifice has meaning, one has to do three things. First of all, one has to ask what were the origins and development of a practice of celebrating the eucharist for particular intentions, and especially of remembering the dead at mass. Secondly, one has to ask why and how did the eucharist become more the act of the ordained priest than the act of the community, and what connection does this have with the first question. Thirdly, it is essential to address the broader issue and to ask in what sense christian tradition interprets the eucharist to be a sacrifice, and what part notions of propitiation have within this development. It is only in the light of such an enquiry that it is possible today to order the celebration of the eucharist with its relation to the forgiveness of sin in mind, and in a way that appropriately includes the remembrance of the living and the dead, encompassing those baptized in Christ beyond the circle of those who gather together.

## Votive Masses

*Votive* is the suitable adjective to use of any eucharistic celebration other than the one dominical eucharist of the gathered faithful, which was in early centuries the primary norm for a community's liturgy. It was indeed a relatively early practice in the church to have special masses alongside the canonically acknowledged authority of one community eucharist in each church.[1] Such masses were celebrated for and by particular groups, at martyrs' tombs, on the occasion of pilgrimages, in remembrance of the dead, and the like. There was also the movement of piety to have weekday celebrations for special groups of people, such as for the clergy of Hippo in

[1] For a survey of different traditions, cf. Robert Taft, 'The Frequency of the Eucharist Throughout History', *Concilium* 152 (Edinburgh & New York: T. & T. Clark & Seabury 1982) 13–24.

Augustine's time.[2] The piety that required more frequent celebration of the mysteries, the cult of martyrs, and the general desire to commemorate the dead in the eucharist, seem to have been three of the principal factors that led to regular celebration outside the weekly community assembly. It is with the third of these that the intensification of the language of offering and sacrifice that drew Trent's attention is most properly associated. The theologians had no trouble in showing that there was a custom of remembering the dead at the eucharist, dating at least as far back as Tertullian, and that the language of offering, sacrifice and propitiation was often associated with this custom. They tended, however, to use patristic citations as proof-texts, instead of seeing both the custom and its sacrificial interpretation in full context.

For example, the text often quoted from Tertullian's *De Corona Militis* reads: 'Oblationes pro defunctis, pro natalitiis annua die facimus'.[3] The quotation occurs in a context in which Tertullian is writing of various practices that are fixed in the life of the church, such as baptism, the eucharist, fasting, and the making of the sign of the cross. Apparently he is referring to eucharistic liturgies for the dead, other than the Sunday assembly. Not too much, however, can be read into the word *oblationes*, which is merely a synonym for eucharist, and having the same broad range of reference as the word *eucharist* itself. Sometimes it refers to the eucharistic celebration as such, sometimes to the bread and wine, sometimes to the anaphora, and sometimes to the sanctified bread and wine. In short, the assertion in the *De Corona* means only this: we do have

---

[2] Cf. Daniel Callam, 'The Frequency of Mass in the Latin Church ca. 400', *Theological Studies* 45 (1984) 613–650.

[3] Tertullian, *De Corona Militis* 3, 3 (Corpus Christianorum, Series Latian II, 1043) Cf. C. Burini, 'Le "oblationes pro defunctis" (Tertulliano, De corona 3, 3)' in *Maranatha: Parola Spirito e Vita* no. 8 (Bologna: Ed. Dehoniane 1983) 254–264.

eucharistic liturgies which we celebrate to mark the passage of the dead to eternal life.

Cyprian, in his first letter, quoted at Trent, objects to the commemoration at the eucharist of one who has caused division in the community, by naming a presbyter as his own tutor.[4] He refers explicitly to the practice of offering the sacrifice for those who fall asleep. The text of the letter indicates that what was done in practice was to have the celebrant name the deceased within the anaphora.[5]

In one of the texts which some of the theologians quoted from John Chrysostom, John's concern is what should be done for sinners who depart this life. He is probably talking of those who though guilty of grave sin have not done canonical penance.[6] His instruction is that such persons should be aided by the prayers, supplications, alms and oblations of the church, and then he explicitly refers to remembering the dead during the celebration of the divine mysteries, when the priest names them at the point at which he prays for all those who have slept in Christ. His sense that this can be of avail even to sinners is illustrated by a comparison with the book of Job: as Job expiated the sins of his children by sacrifice, those who offer for the dead should hope that God will give them some consolation. As can be seen, the comparison is not too sharply drawn. The words *oblation* and *offer* are words that take in the whole eucharistic celebration, and the way in which it could be said that this was done for the dead was to name them at the altar. Moreover, while Job is remembered to have expiated for the sins of his children, this is not said of the eucharistic offering. The point is rather that the remembrance of the dead person by the church at

[4] Cyprian, *Ep.* I, 2 (Corpus Scriptorum Ecclesiasticorum Latinorum III, II) 466.

[5] '. . . neque enim apud altare Dei meretur nominari in sacerdotum prece qui ab altari sacerdotes et ministros voluit avocari.'

[6] John Chrysostom, *In 1 Cor hom. XLII* (PG 61) 361.

the divine mysteries should hold out even greater hope that God will be gracious to the sinner who departs this life.

There was a wide range of texts quoted from Augustine in support of offering the mass for the dead, inclusive of quotations from the *Confessions*, the book on the care of the dead, and the *Enchiridion*. The passages from the *Confessions* concern the death of Augustine's mother, Monica. Here, Augustine mentions the offering of the 'sacrifice of our redemption' as part of the funeral rites.[7] The next chapter offers some explanation of what this entailed, and of the theological thought behind it.[8] The practice is again that of remembering or naming her at the altar. The reason given by Augustine is that though she was a holy person, she still parted this life with her sins and needed God's mercy, as well as protection against the deceits of the devil who will try to bar her way. Her remembrance at the eucharist will be a recall of her own faith in Christ, her own trust that 'her debt has been paid by Christ'.

The *Enchiridion* and the *De Cura pro mortuis gerenda* both refer to the offering of the sacrifice for the dead, bearing out at the same time that this meant their being named by the priest at the altar.[9] It is in the *Enchiridion* in reflecting on the lot of the damned, or on the punishments suffered by those not good enough to enjoy immediate rest in expectation of the resurrection, that Augustine introduces the image of propitiation, meaning by that the alleviation of suffering that the church can obtain through this remembrance and offering.[10]

By and large, if one were to use the distinction invoked at Trent between an offering made *per modum suffragii* and one made *per modum satisfactionis* of these patristic texts, one would

---

[7] Augustine, *Confessions*, Bk. IX, 12.

[8] Bk. IX, 13.

[9] *Enchiridion, sive De fide, spe et caritate* 109–112 (PL 40) 283–284: *De cura pro mortuis gerenda* 1, 3 (PL 40) 593.

[10] *Enchiridion* 112.

have to say that they fall into the category of a remembrance *per modum suffragii*. In remembering Jesus Christ and the saving power of his mysteries, the church relies on this when it remembers and prays for the dead. It is the association of its prayer with the prayer of Christ, its own sharing in his grace, which guarantees the hope that it has for the dead and the confidence in the power of its eucharist. The circle of communion is not closed by death, but the dead and the living share in the same divine mysteries. Just as the living, because joined together in one holy communion, could aid and assist one another on the way of grace, so too the living and the dead help one another. The same law applies here, however, as among the living: the holy avail more for the sinner than the sinner can avail for the holy. Hence, the church learns to give thanks for some of the dead and to turn to them for prayer, while it learns to intercede for others, who, judging from their lives, would appear to still need this assistance.

It was, of course, this notion of propitiation, together with an understanding that doing penance meant making satisfaction, that determined attitudes to the offering of mass in the later middle ages. When dealing with the system of tariff penance, introduced on continental Europe through the influence of celtic monks just before the carolingian era, it is easier to come by facts than it is to get explanations, but the whole idea of having masses offered for the dead is incomprehensible without this background.

The tariff system of penance, as first introduced, provided for the deficiencies of the old canonical, once in a life-time, penance,[11] since it allowed for penance without becoming a public penitent, and allowed for penance and reconciliation more than once in the course of life. It was no easy mode of

[11] For a recent survey of penitentials and the connected penitential system, cf. Allan J. Frantzen, *The Literature of Penance in Anglo-Saxon England* (New Brunswick, N.J.: Rutgers University Press 1983).

remission, since the penances imposed were severe and took years to complete. It was this latter factor in particular which seems to have led to commutations. For example, a year's penance could be performed in twelve days of rigorous mortification, inclusive of harsh fasting, acts of asceticism, and long hours of prayer.[12] These commutations did in time become lighter, and were at times backed up by the willingness of the confessor or of other persons to join the penitent in doing penance. In the end, the principal form of commutation became prayer, and offerings made to monks or clergy to have offices sung and masses said, and this is how the penitential system came to influence mass practice.

Basing his findings on an examination of several european penitentials, Cyrille Vogel has offered this list of commutations as a good example:'[13]

Commutation in the form of masses to be said:

one mass substitutes for seven days of fast
ten masses substitute for four months of fast
twenty masses substitute for seven or nine months of fast
thirty masses substitute for one year of fast

Commutation of cost:

one hundred sous provide for one hundred and twenty masses
one sous provides for one mass
three ounces (of gold?) provide for seven masses
one pound provides for twelve masses.

One can see that such a system would easily provide for a multiplication of mass offerings, and all the more so when it was

[12] Frantzen, op. cit. 55.
[13] Cyrille Vogel, 'Une mutation cultuelle inexpliquée: le passage de l'eucharistie communautaire à la messe privée', *Revue des Sciences Religieuses* 54 (1980) 231–250.

taken as a way of helping the departed in purgatory, who had not done adequate penance in life. Some provided for their own eternal rest by bequest, some came to the help of others in this way. When we read the theology of the fruits of the mass, espoused by someone like Gabriel Biel, already treated in an earlier chapter, we see this whole system explained in terms of the satisfaction offered for sin and the fruits obtained through the offering of mass. That is, however, the final result of the system, and it is not to be presumed that these ideas were the original impulse.

In fact, in the beginning tariff penance appears to have addressed sin and penance from much the same point of view as did canonical penance. The monks found in penance a healing remedy for sin, that both stirred up sorrow and helped to overcome faults. With the shipwreck of one's baptism, one had to obtain the remission of sin by a harder route, and to overcome all the perversions that invade conscience with sin. The binding and loosing of the confessor had to do with the imposition and lifting of penances, the lifting being done when the conversion was deemed achieved. It was a certain leniency in the practice that made penance be seen in a different light. Confessors took into account the severity of leaving penitents unreconciled for a long time and so began to afford reconciliation before the penance was complete. They also put more stress on the shame and sorrow implied in making confession and asked for lighter penances. The leniency was apparently carried even further by the willingness of confessors to do penance with the sinner, or by the appeal to the penances made by others or to the intercession of the saints, who had gone to paradise by the hard way. In all of this, there is a strong note of the communion of saints, of the helps that christians can give to one another in conquering sin and leading decent lives. Still, it left the practice of doing penance unassimilated into an order of things, since remission could now be given before penance, or with only a light penance, leaving open the question as to why penance had to be done at all.

As it so happened, the development of this more private, repeated and easier way of remitting sin, coincided with that great theological movement which sought to explain the whole ordering of society and church in relation to God that is found in scholasticism. The model taken for the ordering of the world was the model of a just order, and the model for understanding humanity's relation to God was that of vassalage. Within this model, sin appeared as a refusal of allegiance to the creator and as disruption of a divinely established order of justice. Great thinkers like Anselm and Thomas Aquinas put the mercy and friendship of God for humankind as the cornerstone of their theologies, but within this mercy they saw remaining the demands of justice. For sin, therefore, satisfaction that repaired injury was required, both making up for injury and restoring right relations. Penances then fitted into the order of satisfaction, and their lightness could be explained by way of the superabundant satisfaction made by Christ, in which human persons did nothing but share when they performed their own penances, under the grace of Christ's headship. If penances done by sinners could already be lightened because backed up by fellow members of the body of Christ, how much more could this apply when it was perceived that they were backed by the death of Christ and his great love for God and for humanity.

Having masses offered for the living and the dead, or providing for masses to be said for oneself after one's demise, easily fitted into this system of thought. In the mass, the sinner could make appeal to the satisfaction made by Christ, or the church in praying for the dead could make appeal to it. This then could be the sense given to the commutation of penances by way of mass-offerings, or to the offering of the mass by the church for the dead. Aquinas had carefully explained that the order of justice envisaged did not depend on the *aequalitas iustitiae* that one finds in a purely human order,[14] and that indeed it is an order without calculation, since the satisfaction made by Christ was superabundant, both because of the quality of the person who made it and because of the excess of his love.[15] Unfortunately, it was a calculating approach to what was originally seen as being without calculation that led to the abuses of the system and the theology of the fruits of the mass. The multiplication of masses, and the oddities surrounding their offering such as a listing of the thirty days of the Gregorian masses or of the number of prayers to be said, are not a necessary part of the explanation that the mass is an appeal for sinners to the satisfactions of Christ. The application made of a mass for a particular person is justified indeed by the appeal made to Christ's satisfaction, but not in the sense that the church has any power of distribution over this, nor in the sense that any calculation of fruits can be made in a matter which by God's grace is beyond calculation. If any use can be made of the term *ex opere operato*, it is only in the sense of comparing the ineffability of the appeal in prayer to Christ's grace with the ineffability of the pouring out of grace in the ministry of the sacraments. Seen this way, the explanation that grace is given through the mass *per modum satisfactionis* is not very different from the *modus suffragii*, since both appeal to the mediation of mercy that is in God's hands alone. The difference really lies in two different images of Christ's mediatorship, the one which sees him as the one who distributes grace, the other as the one who as eternal high-priest intercedes with the Father for grace.

## The Role of the Priest

This last distinction, however, is in its own way tell-tale and can

[14] Thomas Aquinas, *Summa Theologiae* III, Q. XC, art. 2, c.; Supplementum Q. XII, art. 2, c.
[15] Thomas Aquinas, *Summa Theologiae* III, Q. XLVIII, art. 2, c.

have vast implications for the way of understanding the relation between the church and the ordained minister of Christ. If the image of Christ's mediation is that of the eternal high-priest who makes intercession, there is more room left for the Father's gift of the Spirit and for the place of the Spirit in giving graces and charisms to Christ's body. The liturgy is seen as the prayer of Christ, with which the church is associated in the power of the Spirit, and the ministry is a gift that comes from the Spirit, operating in and through the community of faith. If, however, the image of Christ's mediation is that of lord and distributor of grace, then the instrumentality of the priesthood in direct relationship to Christ becomes the controlling model for explaining the place of priesthood in the church. This allows for a greater independency of priestly action from the prayer of the assembly, and gives him at all times and on all occasions the role of public minister, acting in the name of the divinely instituted corporate body.

Like so much else in theology, this latter model of priesthood was offered to explain much that had already come about by practice, and to put some order in worship and sacrament where order had begun to disappear. In re-establishing other practices of church mediation, it is of interest to know what led to the separation of priestly mediation from the prayer of the gathered assembly. The holding of eucharistic assemblies distinct from the Sunday gathering of the church must certainly have had something to do with it, since on such occasions the minister functions less as the leader of a local church and much more as a functionary who could be called upon by the faithful to exercise an office. If someone is ordained to supply the liturgical needs of a place of pilgrimage, such as a martyr's tomb, the image of functionary is heightened.

However, it would be a mistake to ignore the fact that the distinction between priest (as title given first to bishops and then to presbyters) and faithful in the celebration of the eucharist began to show within the Sunday assembly itself quite soon. As early as the time of John Chrysostom and Ambrose, we find bishops lamenting the infrequency of communion on the part of the faithful.[16] In the Gaul of Caesarius of Arles, provisions were made for the departure of a number of the faithful before the communion, since apparently quite a number did not come for that purpose and tended to come and go as they pleased, so that a harassed Caesarius tried to put some order into their going by dismissing non-communicants formally before communion.[17]

Some link the infrequency of communion with the reverence for the divinity of Christ promoted by anti-Arianism. This may have had something to do with it, but does not seem to be the only explanation. One could also relate it to the mystagogy surrounding the eucharist that read the prayer of the presiding bishop as the representation of the heavenly oblation of Christ, the eternal high-priest.[18] Liturgical celebration itself surrounded the anaphora with so much awe and reverence that it became more and more the act of the bishop or other priest, done in Christ's name, and less the great prayer of thanksgiving offered by the assembled church in commemoration of Christ's saving deeds. When in the seventh century Saint Isidore defined the eucharist as *bona gratia*, misconstruing the etymology of the word *eucharistia* to make it mean a grace obtained through the offering of the priest,[19] he was but interpreting a practice whereby the faithful depended less on communion and more on the prayers of the priest. This reliance is not contradicted by the

[16] Cf. Josef Jungmann, *Mass of the Roman Rite*, vol. II (New York: Benziger 1955) 361.

[17] Caesarius of Arles, *Sermones* LXXIII & LXXIV (Corpus Christianorum, Series Latina CIII) 306–312.

[18] E.g., Theodore of Mopsuestia, *Baptismal Homily* IV, 15: english translation in Edward Yarnold, *The Awe-Inspiring Rites of Initiation* (Slough: St. Paul Publications 1971) 219–220.

[19] Isidore of Seville, *Etymologiae* 6, 19, 38 (*Etymologiarum sive Originum* Libri XX: edited by W. M. Lindsay, Oxford: Oxford University Press 1911).

fact that right through the carolingian period theologians wrote of the church itself as the subject that offers the sacrifice, since this is readily enough connected with the concept of the priest as public minister, who acts in the name of the church.[20] Representing the heavenly liturgy of Christ in his earthly liturgy, and acting in the name of the church as public minister, the prayer of the priest becomes the one guarantee of the mercy and grace of God on which the faithful rely more and more, unless they loose interest in it and turn to the saints or to superstitions for their needs and protection. It but takes the phrase *in persona Christi* to allow the church to put more accent on the priest's ministerial power, and less on his prayer, and so to afford him an even greater role in the distribution of grace and the remission of sin.

What is surprising about this turn is that it is so different from the place of a bishop and his helpers in the presidency of local communities in early centuries. In this perspective, the liturgy of the bishop is inseparable from the liturgy of the assembly, gathered in the Spirit and in Christ's name, so that no weight can be attached to it apart from the assembly, even if the liturgy of the assembly is seen to depend on having an ordained minister. This early church perspective, as well as the shift that took place, have been amply documented in research devoted to that precise topic.[21] Here, it is merely necessary to recall the point in order to grasp how different the medieval mass system, and its justification, was from an early liturgy and the remembrance of the dead within that liturgy. Within the system operative at the time, the Council of Trent could define the right and power of an ordained priest to offer mass for the living

[20] Cf. Raphael Schulte, *Die Messe als Opfer der Kirche: die Lehre Frühmittelalterlichen Autoren über das Eucharistische Opfer* (Münster: Aschendorf 1959).

[21] Cf. Hervé Legrand, 'The Presidency of the Eucharist According to Ancient Tradition', *Worship* 53 (1979) 413–438.

and the dead, for sins, satisfactions and other necessities, irrespective of the gathering or non-gathering of the faithful. It could not make of it the traditional ordering of church worship, nor a system that inevitably has to endure.

The whole impulse of the liturgical reform of the Second Vatican Council was to recover a community worship, and together with it the reality and importance of local churches. With this official impulse, there went the spiritual impulse of lived community experiences and liturgies, of a recovery of the power of the Spirit in the church and of a differentiation of ministries. The practice of priestly liturgy and the practice of remembering the dead in the eucharist are changed under this impulse, and the theological explanations are in their turn inevitably modified. The eucharistic sacrifice has to be explained, not as an act of the priest, either in the assembly or outside the assembly for the church as a whole, but as the act of worship of the faithful gathered in the Spirit under the presidency of a minister.

Ecumenical discussion and the effort at agreement has moved the catholic church to an explicit teaching of the sacramental and memorial relation of the eucharist to the cross and to the pasch of Christ. To this extent, the misunderstandings of the sixteenth century that led to seeing mass as an addition to the unique sacrifice of Christ have been cleared away. It has not yet, however, moved the catholic church to any radical change in its official supervision of the exercise of priestly ministry, inclusive of a system of mass offerings, nor to an adequate relocation of the ministry in the assembly, which allows the eucharist to be clearly seen as the worship of the church gathered in faith and love and not as an act of the ordained priest in virtue of a divine power proper to himself and of a public office that he holds by divine institution and transmission.

## 'Sacrifice' and 'Offering' in Eucharistic Discourse

As already pointed out in previous chapters, one of the greatest limits of sixteenth century controversy lay in its undifferentiated use of words such as *sacrifice* and *propitiation*. Having historically relocated the remembrance of the dead in a community liturgy, and having relocated the ministry of the priest within the assembly, it now remains to ask in what sense the use of such terms developed, in an earlier age.

### Liturgical Evidence

Since we are dealing with a liturgical issue, the most obvious thing is to ask how the liturgy itself spoke. In particular, we can look at the evidence of some early eucharistic anaphoras to see how they expressed the meaning of the redemptive work which they commemorated, and how they used the language of sacrifice and offering.

Since the name *anaphora* is itself derived from the greek word meaning 'to offer', it is interesting to note that the earliest examples that we have of probable eucharistic prayers are devoid of the language of offering. This would include the prayer from Didache X, from Book VII of the Apostolic Constitutions, and from the syriac Acts of Thomas.[22] These are straightforward prayers of blessing, expressing thanksgiving, praise and intercession that derive from the memory of Christ and the consciousness of the presence in the community of his Spirit. The anamnesis section, with its mention of offering, becomes standard from our knowledge of the prayer in the *Apostolic Tradition* of Hippolytus onwards. This is the principal point at which the church in prayer interprets its own act as an offering, though other sections of the prayer can also reflect this understanding.

[22] Cf. Cyrille Vogel, 'Anaphores Eucharistiques préConstantiniennes. Formes non traditionnelles', *Augustinianum* 20 (1980) 401–410.

In order not to multiply examples, some quotations are here offered from the Anaphora of Mark of the Alexandrian tradition to give the different senses in which words of sacrifice and offering are customarily used in eucharistic prayers. In the blessing for redemption, this prayer invokes God in the name of Jesus Christ,

> 'though whom with whom and the Holy Spirit we give thanks to thee and offer this reasonable service, this bloodless service, which all the nations offer you, from sunrise to sunset, from south to north, for your name is great among the nations, and in every place incense is offered to your holy name and a pure sacrifice, a sacrifice and offering. . . .[23]

This portion of the text uses Mal 1.11 in a way that is familiar to us from the anti-jewish polemic of such writers as Justin and Irenaeus. In this usage, the writers repudiate Old Testament sacrifices, reflecting on the fact that the christian people's only sacrifice is its prayer of thanksgiving, made in remembrance of Christ and in his name. It is the great thanksgiving itself which is dubbed the church's reasonable service, its pure sacrifice and offering. It is in much this way that we have already seen Tertullian and John Chrysostom speak of the oblation of the church, at which the dead are remembered.

In the intercessions, the Anaphora of Mark recommends to God the offerings in kind made by the faithful, for the needs of the church:

> 'Receive, o God, the thank-offering of those who offer the sacrifices at your heavenly and intellectual altar in the vastness of heaven by the ministry of your archangels; of those who offered much and little, secretly and openly, willingly but unable, and those who offered the offerings today',

[23] The english text of these prayers is taken from R. C. D. Jasper and G. J. Cuming, *Prayers of the Eucharist: Early and Reformed* (New York: Oxford University Press, 2nd edition 1980).

asking that they can be as agreeable to God as were the gifts of Abel, Abraham, and the two mites of the widow in the Gospel story.

In the intercessory part of the prayer, where in this tradition the supper narrative occurs, offering and epiclesis are joined in a prayer which obviously intends that the bread and wine themselves are what the church offers, and over which it invokes the power of the Spirit:

> '... fill this sacrifice with a blessing from you, through the descent of the Holy Spirit ... (there follows the supper narrative)... Proclaiming ... we have offered to you from your own gifts ... send upon these loaves and these cups your Holy Spirit.'

This section of the prayer nicely joins the understanding of the thanksgiving as offering with the offering of the bread and wine, almost as if the offering of the bread and wine consisted in the proclamation over them of the great thanksgiving prayer made in remembrance of God's works, and first and foremost of Jesus Christ. It is by such proclamation and such offering that the church sacramentally participates in the divine mysteries, and with these is joined the offerings made by the faithful for the support and need of the community of the church. This is the way of speech common to all early eucharistic prayers, including the much maligned and acrimoniously disputed Roman Canon. In that prayer, words such as *sacrifice, reasonable service, offering, host,* whether they occur before or after the supper narrative, refer to the community's thanksgiving and intercession, its bread and wine, and the whole liturgical worship which includes the offering of the gifts of the people.[24]

---

[24] On the pertinent Latin vocabulary, cf. David Holeton, 'The Sacramental Language of Saint Leo the Great. A Study of the words "munus" and "oblata" ', *Ephemerides Liturgicae* 92 (1978) 115–165.

The Roman Church therefore indulges in a misinterpretation of its own earliest tradition when in the composition of new eucharistic prayers it presents the section after the supper narrative as an offering of Christ himself, or of his body and blood. The moment perpetuated in this way is the moment of bitter polemic, not the moment of prayerful harmony of early tradition, in the glory of its very diversity.

Another element in eucharistic prayer which deserves attention is the way in which it represents the mystery of Christ and our redemption. Here are some sample quotations:

> 'You took on our human nature to give us life through your divine nature; you raised us from our lowly state; you restored our fall; you restored our immortality; you forgave our debts; you justified our sinfulness; you enlightened our intelligence . . .' (Prayer of Addai and Mari, in the section addressed directly to Christ).
> '. . . he was betrayed to voluntary suffering that he might destroy death, and break the bonds of the devil, and tread down hell, and shine upon the righteous, and fix the limits, and manifest the resurrection' (Prayer from the *Apostolic Tradition*).
> '. . . and he gave himself as a ransom to death, by which we were held, having been sold under sin. By means of the cross he descended into hell, that he might fill all things with himself, and loosed the pains of death; he rose again on the third day, making a way to the resurrection from the dead for all flesh . . .' (Prayer attributed to Basil of Caeserea).

The noteworthy thing about such excerpts is that they are a way of expressing the meaning of those mysteries in which the church participates through the eucharist, or in other words, they express that which is sacramentally represented. It is quite remarkable therefore that there is such little use of sacrificial metaphor to express what is commemorated and shared. Instead, we see a diversity of soteriological imagery, ranging from the harrowing of hell, dwelling place of the devil and of death, to ransom to death itself, to the power of the incarnation and of the resurrection respectively to restore humanity. In face of this kind of liturgical interpretation of redemption, we see how the controversialists of the sixteenth century, both protestant and catholic, confounded themselves by harping on the sacrifice and satisfaction of Christ's death, and thereby limiting the range of sacramental meaning with which he is celebrated in the eucharist.

In the prayer from Book VIII of the *Apostolic Constitutions* we do indeed see the introduction of the new image of propitiation, alongside other images:

'... it pleased him, by your counsel, who was maker of human flesh to become human flesh, the lawgiver to be under the law, the high-priest to be the sacrifice, the shepherd to be the sheep. And he propitiated you, his God and Father, and reconciled you to the world, and freed all from impending wrath. ...'

At the same time, the offering in this prayer governs the bread and wine and the prayer of commemorative thanksgiving, as in the prayers already mentioned:

'Remembering then his passion and death and resurrection from the dead, his return to heaven and his future second coming, in which he comes with glory and power to judge the living and the dead, and to reward each according to their works, we offer you, King and God, according to his commandments, this bread and this cup, giving you thanks through him that you have deemed us worthy to stand before you and be your priests.'

These few texts have been quoted to indicate that it is unfaithful to liturgical tradition either to give too narrow a meaning to sacrificial vocabulary, or to confine the commemorative language in which the work of Christ is remembered to the sacrificial. What is clear from liturgical tradition is that in the eucharistic sacrament the church joins in the prayer of Christ and partakes in his mysteries. This it does through the great thanksgiving prayer, proclaimed over the community's gifts of bread and wine, and through participation in the sacrament of the Lord's Body and Blood, or what Irenaeus calls the 'eucharistized' bread and wine, food and drink of immortality and of the life of the Spirit.

The use of sacrificial imagery and vocabulary has to be seen as one of the church's primary, but not exclusive, ways of interpreting both the death of Christ and the eucharistic sacrament. It is a way of expressing the meaning of the death and our share in it according to the historical imagery available to the early church from the jewish tradition. It is metaphorical language which opens up fresh perceptions of reality by a new use of words. Its power depends on contrast, and like so much else in our language this power can be lost when the contrast is forgotten and words are taken too literally. The contrast of early church usage depended on a process of typology which contrasted type with anti-type, aware of the abyss of difference which lay between the two. It was for christians and non-christians alike a strange and startling use of words to speak of a prayer and of a meal in a house in bread and wine as an offering or a sacrifice, when this language seemed to belong more properly to temple ritual and the sacrificing of animals. It was to allow for the access to God that was opened up to christians through the incarnation and death of Jesus Christ, and which contrasted with other attempts to reach the divine. It was equally strange and startling to speak of Jesus's death as a sacrifice or as a priestly act, endowing thus with dignity a most humiliating execution. It was an essential part of this language to predicate priestliness of the Lord's heavenly intercession, for it was the closeness to God that Christ achieved through his death that was its very aim and that was now made possible in liturgy to his followers.

While using the imagery of sacrifice to interpret Christ's death for themselves, early christian churches did not confine themselves to it. Indeed, its very richness depended on its linking with other images, such as those of witness, ransom, conflict with Satan, the mediation of forgiveness of sins, judgment and the overcoming of death. In a more sinful community, the image of making propitiation to the One whose benefits were being lightly treated appears to have been able to galvanize people to some repentance.

To recapture the awareness that our participation in the eucharist, while being a sacramental sharing in Christ's mystery, is by that very token an interpretation of its meaning and of our communion in it, should help us to face the issues of sacrifice more clearly. How much does that language allow us to grasp and share the meaning of Christ's mysteries and of our common participation in them? How essential is it to such meaning? How much does it have to be completed by other images and ritual expressions? How well does it allow us to express an ethic of participation in Christ and the Spirit in our commitment to God's rule, that is allied to our liturgical prayer? When we prayer and celebrate, are we interpreting life and history, along with our interpretation of the works and sanctification of Jesus Christ, and of the mercy and love of God shown through him for the world?

### Eucharist, Penance, Sin

Our renewal of the language of prayer takes place within a wider context of ecclesial and liturgical change. Since our study has shown us how much the sixteenth century dilemma hinged around a change in mass practice that was associated with a penitential system, some remarks on where we stand today in this regard are appropriate.

First of all, the common mode of participation in the eucharist in the catholic church today is once more that of

183

communion in the Lord's body, and increasingly in his blood. In other words, we do share together at the Lord's table. This has come about with quite extraordinary rapidity, and not without the bemoanings of those who think that it goes against a sense of reverence and of penance, and that it has had effects on the frequency of sacramental confession among the faithful. However, while freedom from sin that alienates was always seen as a necessary condition for joining at the Lord's table, the church's liturgical tradition has from the beginning seen eating and drinking Christ's body and blood as a remedy for sin, not only as an antidote but even as a remission of daily sins. If communion itself once more appears as a communion in God's mercy and healing power, as well as a covenant commitment to the covenant offered in Christ, then having masses said in return for monetary gifts need not be linked to this purpose. The offering of gifts for mutual sustenance or communal needs, for the care of the poor and for the support of those engaged in full-time service to the church's work, whether done in kind or in money, can be restored to their rightful position as the practical side of the church's *koinonia* in the eucharistic celebration. If the language of offering is applied to such deeds, rather than being seen as an offering which is a condition for eucharist and communion, it is an offering which engages us in the gift of life which is offered in the body and blood, by God's initiative.

In the second place, a renewed penitential practice needs to develop along with changes in eucharistic celebration, such as would offer a different context within which to appreciate the relation of the eucharist to the forgiveness of sins and to christian conversion. There are trends in a renewed penitential practice, unhappily all too uncompromisingly treated in the recent Roman Synod, which accentuate the medicinal and disciplinary side of doing penance rather than its satisfactory character. This points to what was in earlier times the most important role of the confessor as healer and counsellor, who aided penitents in finding appropriate ways of overcoming sin through God's grace, and accompanied them on the way of conversion. It also revives some of the communal character of penance, since penance is done as a member of the church community and penitents are helped by the community in seeking reconciliation. Today, we do not separate penitents from the rest of the community, marking some out as those who stand in particular need of the church's help. The commiseration and support offered, however, to certain groups, such as the divorced and remarried, homosexuals, lesbians, drug addicts, alcoholics and single parents, who are struggling with the pressures of contemporary society and its unchartered values, fit into the church's penitential tradition, and need to be given more place within liturgy, in one or other of the forms of our common prayer. We are also more conscious that we all stand together as sinners, needing as a church to face the grave issues of our time which tend to hold humanity far from life and far from God. This has to find expression in fresh ways of doing and celebrating communal penance, but it must also have some effect on our way of sharing eucharist together. In the Lord's Supper, the members of the church come together to share in healing food and drink, in an act of ecclesial reconciliation, and in a mutual strengthening for the struggle against sin and for life, in which christians, despite their individual and communal sinfulness, are called to engage in the public forum. The prayer of remembrance, which is known as a prayer of thanksgiving and praise, is also a prayer for forgiveness, reconciliation and nourishment. It is the pleading of the blood of Christ for mercy, the church's part in the intercession that Christ makes at God's right hand. In this context, what was represented at the Council of Trent as the propitiatory value of the mass can be retrieved and enlarged only by giving attention to all the ways in which the celebration of the eucharist pertains to the forgiveness of sins and the work of reconciliation.

As the Lima statement on the eucharist notes, though in too summary a fashion to take note of all that is in ecclesial tradition, the remembrance of the dead in the mass can be linked with intercession. This does not simply mean that the church makes intercession for them during mass, though it does remind us that the most respected way of remembering them is to mention their names in the eucharistic prayer. More profoundly, it means that in remembering them, the church relies on Christ's intercession, on that heavenly plea to the Father, to whose side he has had access through the shedding of his blood on the cross. We saw in an earlier chapter that this was one of the explanations put forward in the Tridentine debates, but that the notion of satisfaction kept cropping up. Now we recognize how much this category of satisfaction is linked to historical and cultural perceptions of the godly order. Hence we may find that the communion between the living and the dead, and the prayer of the living for the dead, might be best expressed as a shared eschatological hope. Human history has to be redeemed in a common hope, which the living share with past generations. When we intercede for the dead in Christ's name, we are not merely asking for a more comfortable rest for them, but we are giving voice to the realization that our lives are still intimately joined with theirs and that reconciliation and a deepening of communion in Christ's Spirit can take place beyond the separation of the grave.

## Conclusion: Ecumenical Interaction

In the light of the explanation and critique of Trent's dogma on the mass offered in this book, and of the comments made on ecumenical agreements as well as on Roman Catholic teaching today, a few words on the ecumenical exchange which highlights the need for re-reception are appropriate. What appears from the whole discussion is that it is necessary for each church critically and constructively to review its own liturgical and doctrinal tradition. It has to see what is open to challenge in it, to recognize its limitations as well as its fundamental inspirations, asking how it may be received into the life of the church today.

It is imperative in such a review of a sacramental tradition to attend to the unbreakable link between doctrine and practice. A church cannot say that it will keep the doctrine as stated, but change its practice, nor vice versa. This is an impossible fissure. Similarly, in the dialogue between churches, agreement on an appropriate and commonly observed eucharistic practice, within reasonable diversity, is integral to the quest for fuller ecclesial communion. This has indeed been the trend of ecumenical rapprochement, but the closeness of the connection between practices and doctrine needs to be constantly emphasized.

Consequently, the formulation of an appropriate rhetoric, which commands allegiance to agreed practice, and sets the limits within which doctrinal agreement is pursued, is important. To be aware, however, of the precise nature of rhetoric is also important, lest it be expected to carry too much by way of a more abstract doctrinal explanation. For example, *memorial*, as a term to be used, while being central to current ecumenical accord on the Lord's Supper is one that has as much affective appeal as it has cognitive content. Scriptural scholarship alone, to say nothing of philosophies of time and memory, shows how hard it is to unfold the meaning of the word, so that it needs to be accepted as polysemic if it is to serve its ecumenical purpose. If it, or other related formulas such as *effective representation*, are taken as closed formulas, then the situation becomes confused. In recent exchanges, recalled in this work, we seem to have been witness to a clash between the rhetoric of *propitiatory sacrifice* and that of *effective representation* and *anamnesis*. The clash cannot be understood or dealt with, unless the affective, practice-oriented, and heuristic nature of rhetorical language is grasped. Parties who find themselves in disagreement over formulas, have to ask to what diverse eucharistic practices they remain attached, and how much this lies beneath their disagreement over doctrinal formulations. To this extent, perhaps the lutheran observations in *Das Herrenmahl* on the catholic tradition of propitiatory sacrifice and on reformation reactions to it are more to the mark than any of the other remarks about it in recent ecumenical statements. As for the Roman reactions to the *Final Report* of ARCIC, one does not need to be very astute to see how much they serve the preservation of a given image of priesthood and its place in the ordering of the church. As for the catholic suggestion in the dialogue between lutherans and catholics that the church offers Christ as the only acceptable offering, and that in doing this it unites its own self-offering with his, it is clear enough that this was not what the Council of Trent had to say on the mass as sacrifice. Whether it can now be taken as a satisfactory statement can be answered only through a review of the church's traditional use of the language of offering, which is the object of another study and would require another book, that goes beyond the sketchy outline offered in the final chapter of this one.

# Appendix

## ARTICULI ET CANONES

### A. Bologna, 1547

(a)  Articuli haereticorum super missae sacrificio propositi examinandi theologis minoribus (CT VI/1 321–323):

1  Eucharistiam in missa non esse sacrificium nec oblationem pro peccatis sed tantum commemorationem sacrificii in cruce peracti, neque eam offerre esse opus bonum aut meritorium.

2  Missam nec vivis nec mortuis ut sacrificium prodesse, nec aliis applicare posse.

3  Missam non esse ex evangelio neque a Christo institutam, sed inventam ab hominibus questus et lucri causa.

4  Missas privatas illicitas esse atque abrogandas, neque uno die in una ecclesia nisi unam tantum missam celebrandam esse.

5  Non licere sacerdotibus sacrum facere, si non adsint communicantes.

6  Canonem missae abrogandam esse fugiendumque non secus ac pessimam abominationem.

7  Aquam non esse miscendam cum vino in missa, quod ita factum in evangelio non legitur.

(b) Loci haereticorum a Seripando excerpti (CT VI/1 323–325):

1  Missam non esse a Deo institutam.

2  Missam privatam non tollere peccata post baptismum commissa, nec esse sacrificium vel laudis vel satisfactionis, nec impetrare remissionem poenae, nec applicari per eam sanctorum merita ad satisfactionem pro vivis vel pro mortuis.

189

3  Missas privatas illicitas esse nec posse aliis applicari, et
institutas esse, quod teneamus Christum pro originali
peccato satisfecisse, pro aliis autem quotidianis delictis
instituisse missam.

4  Expedire unam tantum missam, quando convenit
populus, in una parochia dici lingua vulgari, reiectoque
canone neque mixta aqua vino.

5  Eucharistiam non esse sacrificium pro peccatis, nec vivis
nec mortuis ut sacrificium prodesse, nec licere eam offerre
ad haec vel illa temporalia impetranda, nec eam offerre esse
bonum obedientiae vel meritorium.

## B. Trent 1551/1552

(a) Articuli haereticorum super missae sacrificio propositi
examinandi theologis minoribus (CT VII/1 375–378):

1  Missam non esse sacrificium nec oblationem pro peccatis,
sed tantum commemorationem sacrificii in cruce peracti,
vocari autem a patribus translato nomine sacrificium; et
vere et proprie non esse, sed tantum testamentum et
promissionem remissionis peccatorum.

2  Missam non esse ex evangelio neque a Christo institutam,
sed inventam ab hominibus; neque eam esse opus bonum
aut meritorium, imo in ea committi manifestam et
multiplicem idololatriam.

3  Blasphemiam irrogari sanctissimo Christi sacrificio in
cruce peracto, si quis credat Dei Filium denuo a
sacerdotibus in missa Deo Patri offerri: Christumque pro
nobis mystice imolari et offerri non aliud esse, quam illum
nobis ad manducandum dari. Et Christum illis verbis: Hoc
facite in meam commemorationem non ordinasse, ut
apostoli offerrent corpus et sanguinem eius in sacrificio
missae.

4 Canonem missae erroribus et seductionibus scatere, abrogandum esse fugiendumque non secus ac pessimam abominationem.

5 Missam nec vivis nec mortuis ut sacrificium prodesse; et impium esse applicare eam pro peccatis, pro satisfactionibus et aliis necessitatibus.

6 Sicut nemo pro aliis communicat vel pro alio absolvitur, ita nec in missa sacerdos pro alio sacrificium offerre potest.

7 Missas privatas, in quibus scilicet solus sacerdos et non alii communicant, ante Gregorium Magnum non fuisse et illicitas esse atque abrogandas; ac cum Christi institutione pugnare et repraesentare magis excommunicationem quam communionem a Christo institutam.

8 Vinum materiam non esse huius sacrificii; neque aquam miscendam cum vino in calice; idque esse contra Christi institutionem.

9 Ecclesiae Romanae ritum, quo secreto et submissa voce verba consecrationis proferuntur, damnandum esse; missamque nonisi in lingua vulgari, quam omnes intelligant, celebrari debere, imposturamque esse certas missas certis sanctis attribuere.

10 In celebratione missarum omnes ceremonias, vestes et externa signa irritabula impietatis esse magis quam officia pietatis. Et sicut missa Christi simplicissima fuit, ita quanto missa illi primae omnium missae vicinior et similior sit, tanto magis esse christianam.

(b) Canones de sacrificio missae examinandi per patres propositi die 18 ianuarii 1552 (CT VII/1 460):

1 Si quid dixerit, in missa non esse sacrificium nec oblationem pro peccatis, sed tantum commemorationem sacrificii in cruce peracti, aut vocari translato nomine sacrificium, et vere et proprie non esse: anathema sit.

2    S.q.d., missam esse tantum testamentum et promissionem remissionis peccatorum: a.s.

3    S.q.d., missae sacrificium non esse ex evangelio nec a Christo institutum, sed inventum ab hominibus, neque illud offerre esse opus bonum aut meritorium, imo in eo committi manifestam et multiplicem idololatriam: a.s.

4    S.q.d., blasphemiam irrogari sanctissimo Christi sacrificio in cruce peracto ab iis, qui Dei Filium a sacerdotibus in missa Deo offerri credunt: a.s.

5    S.q.d., Christum pro nobis mystice in missa imolari et offerri, non aliud esse, quam ipsum nobis ad manducandum dari, aut illis verbis: Hoc facite in meam commemorationem non ordinasse, ut apostoli et alii sacerdotes offerrent corpus et sanguinem eius: a.s.

6    S.q.d., canonem missae erroribus et seductionibus scatere, abrogandum esse fugiendumque non secus ac pessimam abominationem: a.s.

7    S.q.d., missam nec vivis nec mortuis ut sacrificium prodesse, aut impium esse applicare eam pro peccatis, pro satisfactionibus et aliis necessitatibus: a.s.

8    S.q.d., neminem pro alio sacrificium offerre posse, sicut nullus pro alio communicat vel absolvitur: a.s.

9    S.q.d., missas privatas (in quibus videlicet solus sacerdos et non alii communicant, quae diu ante Gregorium Magnum fuere in ecclesia) illicitas esse atque abrogandas et cum Christi instituto pugnare, aut repraesentare magis excommunicationem quam communionem a Christo institutam: a.s.

10    S.q.d., vinum necessariam materiam non esse huius sacrificii neque aquam miscendam esse cum vino in calice, idque esse contra Christi institutionem: a.s.

11    S.q.d., ecclesiae Romanae ritum, quo secreto et submissa voce verba consecrationis proferuntur, damnandum esse, missamque nonnisi in lingua vulgari celebrari debere, ac

imposturam esse certas missas certis sanctis, sicut ecclesia intendit: a.s.

12  S.q.d., ceremonias, vestes et externa signa, quibus in celebratione missarum ecclesia catholic utitur, irritabula impietatis esse magis quam officia pietatis: a.s.

13  S.q.d., missam minus christianam esse, quia cum pluribus ceremoniis celebratur, quam fuerit a Christo celebrata: a.s.

## C. Trent 1562

(a) Articuli tresdecim propositi examinandi theologis minoribus (CT VIII 719):

1  An missa sit sola commemoratio sacrificii in coena peracti, non autem verum sacrificium.

2  An sacrificio in coena peracto deroget sacrificium missae.

3  An illis verbis: Hoc facite in meam commemorationem ordinaverit Christus ut apostoli offerrent corpus et sanguinem suum in missa.

4  An sacrificium, quod in missa fit, prosit solum sumenti, non possit autem offerri pro aliis, tam vivis quam defunctis, nec pro ipsorum peccatis, satisfactionibus et aliis necessitatibus.

5  An missae privatae, in quibus scilicet solus sacerdos et non alii communicant, illicitae sint et abrogandae.

6  An, quod in missa aqua vino admisceatur, cum Christi institutione pugnet.

7  An canon missae errores contineat sitque abrogandus.

8  An ecclesiae Romanae ritus, quo secreto et submissa voce verba consecrationis proferuntur, damnandus sit.

9  An missa nonnisi in lingua vulgari, quam omnes intelligant, celebrari debeat.

10  An abusus sit, certas missas certis sanctis attribuere.

11 An caeremoniae, vestes et signa externa, quibus ecclesia in celebratione missarum utitur, sint tollendae.

12 An Christum pro nobis mystice immolari idem sit, quod nobis ad manducandum dari.

13 An missa sit tantum sacrificium laudis et gratiarum actionis, an etiam sacrificium propitiatorium, tam pro vivis quam pro defunctis.

(b) Canones de sacrificio missae, propositi examinandi (patribus) die 6 augusti 1562 (CT VIII 754f.):

1 Si quis dixerit, missam non esse sacrificium, sed commemorationem tantum sacrificii in cruce peracti. aut vocari translato nomine sacrificium, vere tamen et proprie non esse: a.s.

2 S.q.d., missam tantum esse sacrificium laudis et gratiarum actionis, non autem propitiatorium tam pro vivis quam pro defunctis, nec offerri debere pro peccatis, satisfactionibus et aliis necessitatibus: a.s.

3 S.q.d., blasphemiam irrogari sanctissimo Christi sacrificio in cruce peracto per missae sacrificium aut illi per hoc derogari: a.s.

4 S.q.d., illis verbis: Hoc facite in meam commemorationem non ordinasse Christum, ut apostoli et alii sacerdotes offerrent corpus et sanguinem eius: a.s.

5 S.q.d., sacrificium missae solum prodesse sumenti, non autem posse offerri pro aliis, aut quod offerri non est aliud quam nobis ad manducandum dari: a.s.

6 S.q.d., missas, in quibus solus sacerdos et non alii communicant, illicitas esse et abrogandas: a.s.

7 S.q.d., aquam non miscendam esse cum vino in calice idque esse contra Christi institutionem: a.s.

8 S.q.d., canonem missae erroribus scatere abrogandumque esse: a.s.

9 S.q.d., ecclesiae Romanae ritum, quo secrete et submissa

voce verba consecrationis proferuntur, damnandum esse: a.s.

10  S.q.d., missam nonnisi in lingua vulgari celebrari debere: a.s.

11  S.q.d., imposturam esse, aliquas missas certis sanctis (sicut ecclesia intendit) attribuere: a.s.

12  S.q.d., caeremonias, vestes et externa signa, quibus in missarum celebratione ecclesia catholica utitur, irritabula impietatis esse magis quam officia pietatis: a.s.

(c) (Doctrina et) canones de sacrificio missae, reformata iuxta censuras patrum, et proposita iterum examinanda die 5. septembris 1562, et coepta examinari die 7. (CT VIII 911f.):

1  S.q.d., in missa non offerri Deo verum et proprium sacrificium, aut quod offerre non sit aliud quam nobis Christum ad manducandum dari, vel tantum prodesse sumenti: a.s.

2  S.q.d., missae sacrificium tantum esse laudis et gratiarum actionis, non autem propitiatorium, neque pro vivis et defunctis, pro peccatis et poenis at aliis necessitatibus offerri debere: a.s.

3  S.q.d., illis verbis: Hoc facite in meam commemorationem Christum non instituisse apostolos sacerdotes, aut non ordinasse, ut ipsi aliique sacerdotes offerrent corpus et sanguinem eius: a.s.

4  S.q.d., blasphemiam irrogari smo Christi sacrificio, in cruce peracto, per missae sacrificium, aut ill per hoc derogari: a.s.

5  S.q.d., imposturam esse missas celebrare in honorem sanctorum et pro illorum apud Deum intercessione obtinenda, sicut ecclesia intendit: a.s.

6  S.q.d., canonem missae errores continere ideoque abrogandum esse: a.s.

7  S.q.d., caeremonias, vestes et externa signa, quibus in

missarum celebratione ecclesia catholica utitur, irritabula impietatis esse magis quam officia pietatis: a.s.

8   S.q.d., missas, in quibus solus sacerdos communicat, illicitas esse ideoque abrogandas: a.s.

9   S.q.d., ecclesiae Romanae ritum, quo submissa voce verba consecrationis proferuntur, damnandum esse; aut lingua tantum vulgari missam celebrari debere; aut aquam non miscendam esse vino in calice, eo quod sit contra Christi institutionem: a.s.


(d) ... canones de sanctissimo missae sacrificio, publicati in sessione sexta sacri concilii Tridentini sub Smo D.N. Pio IV Pont. Max. (CT VIII 961f.):

1   Si quis dixerit, in Missa non offerri Deo verum et proprium sacrificium, aut quod offerri non sit aliud quam nobis Christum ad manducandum dari: a.s.

2   S.q.d., illis verbis: Hoc facite in meam commemorationem, Christum non instituisse apostolos sacerdotes, aut non ordinasse, ut ipsi aliique sacerdotes offerrent corpus et sanguinem suum: a.s.

3   S.q.d., missae sacrificium tantum esse laudis et gratiarum actionis, aut nudam commemorationem sacrificii in cruce peracti, non autem propitiatorium; vel soli prodesse sumenti; neque pro vivis et defunctis, pro peccatis, poenis, satisfactionibus et aliis necessitatibus offerri debere: a.s.

4   S.q.d., blasphemiam irrogari sanctissimo Christi sacrificio in cruce peracto per missae sacrificium, aut illi per hoc derogari: a.s.

5   S.q.d., imposturam esse, missas celebrare in honorem sanctorum et pro illorum intercessione apud Deum obtinenda, sicut ecclesia intendit: a.s.

6   S.q.d., canonem missae errores continere ideoque abrogandum esse: a.s.

7   S.q.d., caeremonias, vestes et externa signa, quibus in

missarum celebratione ecclesia catholica utitur, irritabula impietatis esse magis quam officia pietatis: a.s.

8 S.q.d., missas, in quibus solus sacerdos sacramentaliter communicat, illicitas esse ideoque abrogandas: a.s.

9 S.q.d., ecclesiae Romanae ritum, quo submissa voce pars canonis et verba consecrationis proferuntur, damnandum esse; aut lingua tantum vulgari missam celebrari debere; aut aquam non miscendam esse vino in calice, eo quod sit contra Christi institutionem: a.s.

(e) Decretum de observandis et vitandis in celebratione missarum, publicatum in eadem sessione Tridentina sub Pio Papa quarto (CT VIII 962f.):

Atque, ut multa paucis comprehendantur, in primis, quod ad avaritiam pertinet, cuiusvis generis mercedum conditiones, pacta et quidquid pro missis novis celebrandis datur, necnon importunas atque illiberales eleemosynarum exactiones potius quam postulationes aliaquae huiusmodi, quae a simoniaca labe vel certe a turpi quaestu non longe absunt, omnino prohibeant.

# SELECTED BIBLIOGRAPHY

## Primary Sources

Anglican-Roman Catholic International Commission, *The Final Report* (London: SPCK 1982).

Concilium Tridentinum: *Diariorum, Actorum, Epistularum, Tractatuum Nova Collectio*, edited by the Societas Goerresiana (Freiburg im Breisgau: Herder & Co. 1901–) vols. VI/1, VI/2, VII/1, VII/2, VIII.

*The Book of Concord: Confessions of the Evangelical Lutheran Church*, translated and edited by Theodore G. Tappert (Philadelphia: Fortress 1976).

Congregation for the Doctrine of the Faith, 'Observations on the Final Report of ARCIC', *The Tablet* 236 (1982) 492–495.

——, 'Epistula de Ministro Eucharistiae', AAS LXXV (1983) 1004–1009: English text in *Origins* 13 (1983) 229–230.

Faith and Order Paper No. 111, *Baptism, Eucharist and Ministry* (Geneva: WCC 1982).

Gemeinsame Römische-Katholische/Evangelisch-Lutheranische Kommission, *Das Herrenmahl* (Paderborn: Bonifacius 1978), translated as

Lutheran/Roman Catholic Joint Commission, *The Eucharist* (Geneva: The Lutheran World Federation 1980).

*Growth in Agreement: Reports and Agreed Statements of Ecumenical Conversations on a World Level*, edited by Harding Meyer and Lukas Vischer (New York: Paulist & Geneva: WCC 1984).

John Paul II, 'Dominicae Cenae: Epistula de SS. Eucharistiae Mysterio et Cultu', *Notitiae* XVI (1980) 125–154: English text in *The Pope Speaks* 25 (1980) 139–164.

## Secondary Literature

Acerbi, Antonio, 'Receiving Vatican II in a Changed Historical Context', *Concilium* 146 (Edinburgh: T. & T. Clark, and New York: Seabury 1981) 77–84.

Bäumer, Remigius, *Von Konstanz nach Trient: Beiträge zur Geschichte der Kirche von den Reformkonzilien bis zum Tridentinum* (München-Paderborn-Wien: Ferdinand Schöningh 1972).

Bossy, John, 'Essai de sociographie de la messe, 1200–1700', *Annales. Economies, Sociétés, Civilisations* 36 (1981) 44–70.

Brilioth, Yngve, *Eucharistic Faith and Practice: Evangelical and Catholic* (London: SPCK 1930. Reprint 1965).

Burini, C., 'Le "oblationes pro defunctis" (Tertulliano, De corona 3, 3)' in *Maranatha: Parola Spirito e Vita* no. 8 (Bologna: Ed. Dehoniane 1983) 254–264.

Callam, Daniel, 'The Frequency of Mass in the Latin Church ca. 400', *Theological Studies* 45 (1984) 613–650.

Christian, William A., *Local Religion in Sixteenth-Century Spain* (Princeton: Princeton University Press 1981).

*Il Concilio di Trento e la Riforma Cattolica. Atti del Convegno Storico Internazionale Trento 2–6 settembre 1963* (Roma 1965).

*Confessing One Faith: A Joint Commentary on the Augsburg Confession by Lutheran and Catholic Theologians*, edited by George W. Forell & James F. McCue (Minneapolis: Augsburg 1982).

*Confessio Augustana und Confutatio: der Augsburger Reichstag 1530 und die Einheit der Kirche*, in Verbindung mit Barbara Hellensleben herausgegeben von Erwin Iserloh (Münster: Aschendorf 1980).

Congar, Yves, 'La "Réception" comme réalité écclésiologique', *Revue des Sciences Philosophiques et Théologiques* 56 (1972).

Davis, Natalie Z., 'The Sacred and the Body Social in 16th

Century Lyon', *Past and Present* 90 (1981) 40–70.

*L'Ecclesiologia del Vaticano II: Dinamismi e Prospettive*, a cura di G. Alberigo (Bologna: Ed. Dehoniane 1981).

Fransen, Piet, 'Réflexions sur l'anathéme au Concile de Trente', *Ephemerides Theologicae Lovaniensis* XXIX(1953) 657–672.

Frantzen, Allen J., *The Literature of Penance in Anglo-Saxon England* (New Brunswick N.J.: Rutgers University Press 1983).

Galpern, A. N., *The Religion of the People in Sixteenth-Century Champagne* (Cambridge: Cambridge University Press 1976).

Heron, Alasdair I. C., *Table and Tradition: Toward an Ecumenical Understanding of the Eucharist* (Philadelphia: Westminster Press 1983).

Holeton, David, 'The Sacramental Language of Saint Leo the Great. A Study of the words "munus" and "oblata" ', *Ephemerides Liturgicae* 92 (1978) 115–165.

Holstein, Henri, 'La Cène et la Messe dans la doctrine du sacrifice eucharistique du Concile de Trente', in *Humanisme et Foi Chrétienne* (Paris: Beauchesne 1976) 649–662.

Huels, John M., 'Trent and the Chalice: Forerunner of Vatican II?', *Worship* 56 (1982) 386–400.

Iserloh, Erwin, 'Der Wert der Messe in der Diskussion der Theologen vom Mittelalter bis zum 16. Jahrhundert', *Zeitschrift für katholische Theologie* 83(1961) 44–79.

Jamouelle, E., 'L'unité sacrificielle de la Cène, la Croix et l'Autel au Concile de Trente', *Ephemerides Theologicae Lovaniensis* XXII(1946) 34–69.

——, 'Le sacrifice eucharistique au Concile de Trente', *Nouvelle Revue Théologique* 67 (1945) 1121–1139.

Jasper, R. C. D. & G. J. Cuming (eds.), *Prayers of the Eucharist: Early and Reformed* (Oxford & New York: Oxford University Press, 2nd edition 1980).

Jedin, Hubert, *Geschichte des Konzils von Trient*, vols. III & IV/1

(Freiburg im Breisgau: Herder 1970/1975).

Lamb, Matthew, *Solidarity With Victims: Toward a Theology of Social Transformation* (New York: Crossroad 1982).

Lepin, Maurice, *L'Idée du Sacrifice de la Messe d'après les Théologiens depuis l'Origine jusqu'à Nos Jours* (Paris: Beauchesne 1926).

Lonergan, Bernard, *Method in Theology* (London: Darton Longmann & Todd 1971).

Oakley, Francis, *The Western Church in the Later Middle Ages* (Ithaca & London: Cornell University Press 1979).

Ozment, Steven, *The Reformation in the Cities: the Appeal of Protestantism to Sixteenth-Century Germany and Switzerland* (New Haven & London: Yale University Press 1975).

———, *The Age of Reformation 1250–1550: An Intellectual and Religious History of Late Medieval and Reformation Europe* (New Haven & London: Yale University Press 1980).

———, (ed.), *Reformation Europe: A Guide to Research* (St. Louis: Center for Reformation Research 1982).

Taft, Robert, 'The Frequency of the Eucharist Throughout History', *Concilium* 152 (Edinburgh: T. & T. Clark, and New York: Seabury 1982) 13–24.

Van Beeck, Frans, *Christ Proclaimed: Christology as Rhetoric* (New York: Paulist 1970).

Voegelin, Eric, *The Ecumenic Age*, vol. 4 of *Order in History* (Baton Rouge: Louisiana State University Press 1974).

Vogel, Cyrille, 'Anaphores Eucharistiques pré-Constantiniennes', *Augustinianum* 20 (1980) 401–410.

———, 'Une mutation cultuelle inexpliquée: le passage de l'eucharistie communautaire à la messe privée', *Revue des Sciences Religieuses* 54 (1980) 231–250.

Wicks, Jared, 'Abuses under Indictment at the Diet of Augsburg 1530', *Theological Studies* 41 (1980) 253–321.

# ANNOTATED BIBLIOGRAPHY FOR FURTHER READING

## Ecumenical Conversations

Anglican-Roman Catholic International Commission, *The Final Report* (London: SPCK 1982).

Lutheran/Roman Catholic Joint Commission, *The Eucharist* (Geneva: The Lutheran World Federation 1980).

These two joint ecumenical statements are good examples of an *anamnesis* approach to a resolution of sixteenth century debates between catholics and reformers. The latter also has a number of supplementary studies by German scholars which put the questions into good historical perspective.

*Growth in Agreement: Reports and Agreed Statements of Ecumenical Conversations on a World Level*, edited by Harding Meyer and Lukas Fischer (New York: Paulist, & Geneva: WCC 1984).

This work presents a number of agreed statements on the eucharist. Besides the above two, noteworthy are the Roman Catholic/Methodist and the Roman Catholic/Presbyterian dialogues.

Faith and Order Paper No. 111, *Baptism, Eucharist and Ministry* (Geneva: WCC 1982).

Known as the *Lima Statement*, this statement issued by the Faith and Order Commission of the World Council of Churches has become a point of reference in ongoing ecumenical dialogue.

John Paul II, 'Letter on the Eucharist', *The Pope Speaks* 25 (1980) 139–164.

Known by its first words *Dominicae Cenae*, this is the best consulted current statement of Roman Catholic magisterial teaching on the eucharist, including the issues of sacrifice and the priestly ministry.

Heron, Alasdair I. C., *Table and Tradition: Toward an Ecumenical Understanding of the Eucharist* (Philadelphia: Westminster Press 1983) 146–175.

These pages give a good survey of what points of agreement have been reached between the catholic and reformation churches, and of what problems are still outstanding.

## The Sixteenth Century Debates and the Council of Trent

Davis, Natalie Zemon, 'From "Popular Religion" to Religious Cultures', in Steven Ozment (ed.), *Reformation Europe: A Guide to Research* (St. Louis Centre for Reformation Research 1982) 321–336.

Oakley, Francis, 'Religious and Ecclesiastical Life on the Eve of the Reformation', in Ozment, op. cit. 5–22.

Oakley, Francis, *The Western Church in the Later Middle Ages* (Ithaca and London: Cornell University Press 1979) 82–130.

These three studies give a good overview of religious devotion and practice before, and at the time of, the reformation, and thus provide an important background for an understanding of the issues at stake between catholics and reformers.

Clark, Francis, *Eucharistic Sacrifice and the Reformation* (London: Darton, Longmann & Todd 1960).

Written from a biased anti-reformation stance, this book nonetheless gives useful information on the catholic theology of the mass in the sixteenth century and on the positions of the reformers.

Obermann, Heiko, *Forerunners of the Reformation: The Shape of Late Medieval Thought Illustrated by Key Documents* (Philadelphia: Fortress 1981) 241–267.

These pages present the thought of two leading catholic apologists, Cajetan and Sylvester Prierias.

Wicks, Jared, 'Abuses under Indictment at the Diet of Augsburg 1530', *Theological Studies* 41 (1980) 253–321.

This article is an excellent survey of the issues at stake at an early stage of the reformation debate, and of the positions taken by both sides.

Iserloh, Erwin and Vilmos Vajta, 'The Sacraments: Baptism and the Lord's Supper', in *Confessing One Faith: A Joint Commentary on the Augsburg Confession by Lutheran and Catholic Theologians*, edited by George W. Forell and James F. McCue (Minneapolis: Augsburg 1982) 2.

How two leading scholars now see the historical issues.


## Other Works

Daly, Robert J., *The Origins of the Christians Doctrine of Sacrifice* (Philadelphia: Fortress 1978).

A shortened version of another study, this work gives a good survey of the uses of sacrificial language in the bible and in the literature of the early church.

Young, Frances M., *Sacrifice and the Death of Christ* (London: SPCK 1975).

The author examines the significance of sacrifice in the pagan religions, in the Old Testament and in early christian literature, and draws consequences for a theology of redemption and of worship today.

Schulz, H.-J., 'Patterns of Offering and Sacrifice', *Studia Liturgica* 15 (1982/83) 34–48.

Stevenson, Kenneth, ' "Anaphoral Offering": Some Observations on Eastern Eucharistic Prayers', *Ephemerides Liturgicae* 94 (1980) 209–288.

These two essays survey the usage of early eucharistic prayers.

# SUBJECT INDEX

Anaphora, offering, 177–182.
See Canon Missae, Eucharistic Prayer
Anathema, meaning of,
126–128

Canon Missae, 51, 53, 65, 67,
91
Codex Iuris Canonici, xii
Confessio Augustana, 29f, 55
—Apologia, 46, 48f
—Confutatio, 45
Congregation for the Doctrine
of the Faith, xi, 18, 21, 23,
24, 132
*Corinthians*, use of at Trent, 59,
91, 99, 119
Cross, and Mass, 45–47, 69–76,
86, 119, *passim*

Dogma
—and imperatives of faith,
154–161
—interpretation of,
136–161
—as meaning, 138–146
—re-reception of, 136–138
—and symbol, 150–154
—as worship, 146–150

Ecumenical Conversations and
Agreements, 1–21
—ARCIC, xi, 3, 9, 10, 14,
17, 132
—Faith and Order (Lima),
xi, 1, 7, 8, 9, 13, 16, 19

—Lutheran/Roman Catholic, 2, 4, 6, 7, 17, 18,
132
—Methodist/Roman
Catholic, 2, 3, 9, 12, 13,
17
—Reformed/Roman
Catholic, 11, 17
*Ex opere operato*, 5f, 29–31, 41,
45, 47, 49, 56–58, 74, 78, 79,
81, 84, 131, 158f
Eucharistic Prayer, 15–17. See
Anaphora

Fruits of Mass, 63, 80–82,
*passim*

*Genesis* 14, 18, use of at Trent,
86f, 101. See Melchisedech
Heavenly Priesthood of Christ
and Mass, 76–82, 101
*Hebrews*, use of at Trent, 59,
69, 77, 86f, 99, 101

*In persona Christi*, xi, 22, 23, 24,
25, 56, 73

John Paul II, teaching of, ix,
21–23, 132, 134

Last Supper, and Mass, xi, 45,
49, 76–82, 86–88, 99–102,
105–114

*Malachi* 1, 10f, use of at Trent,